COUNTRY DIAGNOSTIC STUDY ON LONG-TERM CARE IN THAILAND

DECEMBER 2020

ASIAN DEVELOPMENT BANK

ADB

© 2020 Asian Development Bank
6 ADB Avenue, Mandaluyong City, 1550 Metro Manila, Philippines
Tel +63 2 8632 4444; Fax +63 2 8636 2444
www.adb.org

Some rights reserved. Published in 2020.

ISBN 978-92-9262-550-4 (print); 978-92-9262-551-1 (electronic); 978-92-9262-552-8 (ebook)
Publication Stock No. TCS200373-2
DOI: http://dx.doi.org/10.22617/TCS200373-2

The views expressed in this publication are those of the authors and do not necessarily reflect the views and policies of the Asian Development Bank (ADB) or its Board of Governors or the governments they represent.

ADB does not guarantee the accuracy of the data included in this publication and accepts no responsibility for any consequence of their use. The mention of specific companies or products of manufacturers does not imply that they are endorsed or recommended by ADB in preference to others of a similar nature that are not mentioned.

By making any designation of or reference to a particular territory or geographic area, or by using the term "country" in this document, ADB does not intend to make any judgments as to the legal or other status of any territory or area.

Please contact pubsmarketing@adb.org if you have questions or comments with respect to content, or if you wish to obtain copyright permission for your intended use that does not fall within these terms, or for permission to use the ADB logo.

Corrigenda to ADB publications may be found at http://www.adb.org/publications/corrigenda.

Notes:
In this publication, "$" refers to United States dollars.
ADB recognizes "China" as the People's Republic of China.

On the cover: Due to the rapidly aging population in Thailand, there is an increased urgency to develop care and support systems for older persons (photos from ADB Photo Library).

Printed on recycled paper

CONTENTS

TABLES AND FIGURES

FOREWORD

Rapid aging in Asia and the Pacific has put the region at the forefront of one of the most important global trends. The demographic shift is largely the result of both increased longevity and decreased fertility rates, which are both examples of development success. The change is happening at an unprecedented pace: in 2020, 13% of the population in the Asia and Pacific region is aged 60 or above, and by 2050, it is expected to increase to 24%, or roughly 1.3 billion people. At the same time, traditional family support systems are weakening due to increased migration, urbanization, decreasing family sizes, and expanding female labor market participation. Even when family care support is available, people with complex care needs and their caregivers require additional support.

The demographic, economic, and social trends are resulting in a growing need to establish and finance long-term care (LTC) services and develop the enabling environments to support older people to age well and help families and communities to care for their older citizens. The development of models of care that are affordable, sustainable, accessible, efficacious, and adapted to local contexts is sorely needed.

The window of opportunity to plan for, prepare, and adapt to the needs of aging populations is now. There is great diversity among countries in the region. Some are aging at a fast rate and need to adapt quickly, others will age slower, but will end up with very large older populations. What is common, however, is that countries in the region will see change in the coming years and need to prepare for it. The coronavirus disease (COVID-19) pandemic and its disproportionate impacts on older persons and on existing care systems have illustrated how important it is to strengthen existing systems and develop new capacities.

The Asian Development Bank (ADB) has a growing portfolio on LTC, and is working to capitalize on opportunities of increased population longevity and help mitigate the social and fiscal risks of population aging. In May 2016, ADB approved the regional capacity development technical assistance for the Strengthening Developing Member Countries' Capacity in Elderly Care project, to help increase the capacity of developing member countries to design policies and plans for the improvement of their LTC services. The six diverse countries included in this regional technical assistance are Indonesia, Mongolia, Sri Lanka, Thailand, Tonga, and Viet Nam.

The technical assistance aims to (i) build a knowledge base in the region for the development of LTC systems and services; (ii) improve the capacity of officials and other stakeholders in these countries to design and implement strategic LTC plans; and (iii) create a network for disseminating knowledge, good practices, and expertise.

This country diagnostic study aims to help strengthen the knowledge base on emerging LTC policies, programs, and systems in Thailand. The study outlines findings on the current situation of LTC with regard to the need for care and the supply of care, regulatory and policy frameworks, service provision, quality management, human resources, and financing. Analysis, conclusions, and recommendations concerning LTC system development are also included and have been informed by an in-country consultative process.

Population aging is a key megatrend of the 21st century, and how the Asia and Pacific region adapts to this trend will be an important factor in the continued development of the region. ADB is committed to working with our members on this journey.

Woochong Um
Director General
Sustainable Development and Climate Change Department
Asian Development Bank

ACKNOWLEDGMENTS

This publication was prepared under the regional technical assistance for Strengthening Developing Member Countries' Capacity in Elderly Care project (TA 9111) by the Social Development Thematic Group of the Asian Development Bank (ADB). The report is one of six country diagnostic assessments—done for Indonesia, Mongolia, Sri Lanka, Thailand, Tonga, and Viet Nam—that examine existing elderly care policies, services, and systems, including identification of gaps and opportunities toward long-term care development. Wendy Walker, chief of the Social Development Thematic Group, Sustainable Development and Climate Change Department, provided overall guidance and technical advice to the study, with support from Yukiko Ito, Imelda Marquez, Rizza Loise Aguilar-Crisanto, and Maria Genieve Edar. ADB colleagues from the Human and Social Development Division of the Southeast Asia Department gave strong support by providing insights and feedback throughout the implementation of TA 9111 in-country activities in Indonesia, Thailand, and Viet Nam, including Ayako Inagaki, director; Sakiko Tanaka, principal social sector specialist; Azusa Sato, social sector specialist; and Ye Xu, health specialist. We also would like to thank Thailand Resident Mission's Hideaki Iwasaki, country director; James Roop, principal country specialist; and the rest of the team for providing valuable comments in finalizing the report.

The Thailand country diagnostic study has been a collective effort, and ADB extends its gratitude to the TA 9111 national consultants who contributed to the completion of the diagnostic report: Associate Professor Siriphan Sasat, Chulalongkorn University; and Thawon Sakunphanit, policy and planning analyst. ADB is thankful to HelpAge International's team of consultants, consisting of Meredith Wyse, team leader; and Wendy Holmes, international elderly care health specialist, for helpful comments throughout the process of conducting the study; and Usa Khiewrord, Caitlin Littleton, Peter Morrison, Tassannee Surawana, and Rachanichol Arunoprayote for administering and guiding the diagnostic study team.

The financial support provided by the Japan Fund for Poverty Reduction and the Republic of Korea e-Asia and Knowledge Partnership Fund, both administered by ADB, is acknowledged with gratitude.

ABBREVIATIONS

ADB	Asian Development Bank
ADL	activities of daily living
B	Thai baht (national currency)
B.E.	Buddhist Era
DHSS	Department of Health Service Support (Ministry of Public Health)
ESCAP	Economic and Social Commission for Asia and the Pacific (United Nations)
HCVE	Home Care Volunteers for the Elderly
HISRO	Health Insurance System Research Office
IADL	instrumental activities of daily living
ILO	International Labour Organization
IOM	International Organization for Migration
LAO	local administration organization
LTC	long-term care
LTOP	Long-Term Care Service Development for the Frail Elderly and Other Vulnerable People
MMSE	Mini-Mental State Examination
MOC	Ministry of Commerce
MOF	Ministry of Finance
MOPH	Ministry of Public Health
MSDHS	Ministry of Social Development and Human Security
NCE	National Committee on the Elderly
NESDB	National Economic and Social Development Board
NGO	nongovernment organization
NHA	National Health Accounts
NHES	National Health Examination Survey
NHSO	National Health Security Office
NSO	National Statistical Office
OIC	Office of Insurance Commission
RAP	Rapid Assessment Protocol
SCCT	Senior Citizens Council of Thailand
SSS	Social Security Scheme
TEPHA	Thai Elderly Promotion and Health Care Association
UCS	Universal Coverage Scheme
VHV	village health volunteer
WHO	World Health Organization

EXECUTIVE SUMMARY

This report aims to depict the current situation of long-term care (LTC) of older persons in Thailand, analyze key gaps in the LTC system, and make recommendations to improve LTC in the country.

Context

A drop in fertility rates and increased life expectancies are dramatically changing the age structure of the population in Thailand. Thailand is a rapidly aging society, as 16.7% of its population was over the age of 60 in 2017, and that figure is projected to rise to 32% by 2040. Recent economic growth has slowed, and is projected to remain low due to structural challenges, low productivity, and the aging society. Poverty and inequality are continuing problems for Thailand, with 9.9% of its population (6.7 million) living below the poverty line in 2018.[1]

This shift in Thailand's demographics is causing shifts in the needs of the population, and one of these is an increasing need for care support. Multimorbidities and conditions such as dementia are more common among the older population, increasing the complexity of their care needs. While not all older persons have care support needs, a higher proportion of older persons experience a significant loss of physical and/or mental capacity, a trend that increases with advancing age. Several estimates on the need for care have been undertaken, and they suggest that about 1.5%–2.0% of older persons have severe dependency needs, about 8% need assistance to overcome their limitations, and a much higher percentage (more than 35%) experience some functional limitations that they manage on their own. Investments of effort and resources in health maintenance, disease prevention, and self-care over the course of an individual's life could reduce the need for care later on. As is true in most countries, **the family has been the main or sole caregiver for older members with functional limitations**. However, an increase in the number of older persons, a decrease in the number of adult children, increased migration for work, and increased female participation in the labor force are all reducing the capacity of the family to provide care for their older members. Family caregivers often experience stress, difficulties with their own health, and other challenges. Additionally, some older persons have complex care needs that family caregivers cannot handle. As the status quo reliance on informal caregivers is no longer sufficient, the further development of the country's LTC system has emerged as a priority.

Since the beginning of the century, Thailand has taken several steps toward adapting to an aging population. The current National Plan for Older Persons 2001–2021 is being implemented by the Older Persons' Council. Compliant with international requirements, it uses a life-course planning approach,

[1] The coronavirus disease (COVID-19) pandemic is expected to increase Thailand's poverty incidence to as high as 16% in 2020. COVID-19 Active Response and Expenditure Support Program: Summary Poverty Reduction and Social Strategy. https://www.adb.org/sites/default/files/linked-documents/54177-001-sprss.pdf.

under which (i) older persons should live with their families and in their communities; (ii) public welfare services should meet the needs of older persons who cannot stay with their families or in their communities and maintain an acceptable quality of life; and (iii) the rights of older persons should be protected, especially from abuse, neglect, and violence. Thailand has a universal old-age allowance of B600–B1,000 per month, depending on the age, as well as universal health coverage through three main insurance schemes: the Civil Servant Medical Benefit Scheme (for civil servants, active and retired, and their dependents), the Social Security Scheme (for employees of private companies), and the Universal Coverage Scheme (UCS) (for everyone else). The Ministry of Social Development and Human Security provides additional assistance, including shelter, temporary financial aid, and grants for home modifications, depending on need. The Government of Thailand is committed to age-friendly and accessible housing, buildings, and public spaces, but implementation has been slow.

Thailand has made significant progress toward developing an LTC system, which it is working to strengthen, expand, and improve. In 2009, Thailand developed a national definition for LTC that refers to all the dimensions of care, including the social, health, economic, and environmental aspects. It states that LTC is needed by older persons who have difficulties due to chronic disease or disability, and who are partially or totally dependent on others for the activities of daily living. Thailand's conceptual framework for LTC is contained in the concept of "active aging." For older persons with a degree of dependency, aging in place remains the priority, and care services and other measures either already exist or are being developed to enable that.

The government, recognizing the growing care needs of the population, is following a step-by-step approach to the development of care services. It has chosen to begin by increasing the availability of home-based support for older persons with high care needs through a pilot program managed by the National Health Security Office and local authorities. The program provides 2–8 hours of home-based care support a week, depending on need. Established in 2016, it has built upon a decade of trials of various models for home- and community-based care, with an emphasis on services provided at home. Since 2018, the project has had a budget of B1.25 billion, and has targeted 193,000 older persons. It operates through a care-management system, providing home-based care through caregivers with 70 hours of training, who are supervised by a care manager. The system includes individualized care assessments and care planning. If an older person meets the eligibility criteria, social services may provide assistance with housework, activities of daily living, the provision of assistive devices, and activities outside the house. Medical services, including preventive services, physiotherapy, and the provision of rehabilitative and assistive devices, are also available for dependent older persons through the LTC pilot program and the universal health coverage package. The program provides an interesting case study for other low- and middle-income countries looking for feasible, integrated home- and community-based care models.

Residential LTC is intended for those with complex care needs and insufficient caregiving support at home. Residential care services for dependent older persons are available at private nursing homes, private hospitals, government residential homes, and homes for poor older persons supported by charitable organizations. These facilities provide services ranging from basic to complex care. Such care facilities are increasing, with 442 private facilities in 2016, according to the government's Department of Business Development. With the exception of a limited number of public welfare residential homes, the government has identified its role in residential care as primarily that of a regulator.

The care workforce is a key concern with regard to the quality of LTC in Thailand. The country has an established history of health volunteers from which to build on, some of whom have received caregiving training. In 2018, about 75% of the institutions participating in the national pilot home-based LTC program used volunteers, although the initial evaluation of the scheme found that paid caregivers performed better. There are no large numbers of trained paid caregivers in Thailand, however, and the current health and social welfare staff have neither sufficient training nor an integrated approach for responding to those with care needs. Medical specialists and other care professionals are also underqualified in LTC. There is some work underway to improve and standardize training and professional-certification programs, and to improve quality-management protocols for private and public sector care providers, but there has been little discussion on how to best support family caregivers.

Thailand has no overall governing body responsible for LTC, though the Ministry of Public Health, the Ministry of Social Welfare, the Ministry of Finance, the Ministry of Interior, and the Office of the Insurance Commission all have different responsibilities related to LTC. Challenges remain in implementing the necessary coordination between the related agencies, as required by the relevant legislation.

Families are a major source of financing for LTC in Thailand, both through the provision of unpaid labor and for their out-of-pocket payments for health and care services. Government revenue is the source of financing for the pilot home-based LTC program, and the UCS finances some elements of LTC provision. The National Health Security Office's Fund Management Manual of National Health Security (2019) estimated the budget for LTC at B916.8 million for fiscal year 2019 (ended September 2019).

The cost of care in a public residential facility is significantly higher than that of home-based care; and private facilities, as well as other facilities that provide nursing care, are even more expensive. Demand for residential-facility LTC is likely to increase, so private LTC facilities may need soft loans for capital investment in order to adhere to the official standards and practices. Older persons and families also need financial mechanisms for mitigating the risk of catastrophic expenditure due to LTC, such as specific saving policies or LTC insurance.

Several attempts to estimate the future costs of LTC have been made in Thailand. One earlier projection estimated that if 2% of older persons with severe dependency received residential care, the cost would be B908 million in 2009 and would rise to B2,766 million by 2024. A second projection estimated that universal coverage for community-based LTC for only those with severe dependency would cost 0.6%–1.1% of government revenue and about 0.16%–0.22% of gross domestic product. Investing in LTC system development may add to the gross domestic product, for instance through the impacts on workforce participation (particularly by women and older persons), the demand for LTC-related services, and the demand for assistive devices and other care products.

Discussion and Conclusions

Thailand has made more progress on LTC than most low- and middle-income countries in the region. A key strength of the Thai approach to LTC system development is the investment in, and use of, research and evidence to inform policy and program design, supported by advocacy efforts by a wide range of stakeholders. Secondly, the national definition of LTC and emphasis on aging in place have helped guide a step-by-step approach to LTC system coverage, as they underlie the policy of starting with the development and expansion of home- and community-based care support.

Nevertheless, there are many challenges to overcome as Thailand works to establish a comprehensive, quality, and integrated LTC system that ensures that the care needs of its population are met. There is an urgent need to clarify the division of responsibilities for coordination and governance among the key government agencies and between the central and local authorities. Registration, regulation, national care standards, and accompanying legislation need to be developed and implemented in order to progress toward quality management of both public and private care.

While emphasizing home- and community-based care is an efficient choice, there may be gaps in care, particularly for those with severe care needs. The lack of care provision for those with severe care needs is an important element to consider in planning. The public welfare residential institutions are de facto providers of care due to their residents' developing care needs while living there, but there have been no plans to develop this function any further. It is important that all parties work to provide person-centered care and to help older persons attain the best quality of life possible—at home with the family, through community support, or, when necessary, in residential care.

Shortages in the care workforce are a serious concern, so there should be a long-term plan to ensure that sufficient human resources are generated to meet the growing demand for care. Financing LTC will continue to be a challenge for Thailand, and an LTC insurance system will likely be needed. An expansion of the government's pilot home-based LTC program will require a reexamination of the program's financing. It is currently supported through general public revenues, and is only available to the 70% of the population that is covered by the UCS, with no option for others to buy any services. Local taxes or tax transfers may also be needed to finance the social support elements of LTC, as the UCS expands to include more health-related LTC services.

I. BACKGROUND AND CONTEXT

The Asian Development Bank (ADB) has a growing portfolio of long-term care (LTC) projects, and is engaging in the sector to help mitigate the risk of substantial fiscal constraints and the negative social consequences due to aging. In May 2016, ADB approved regional technical assistance for the Strengthening Developing Member Countries' Capacity in Elderly Care project, to encourage the development of plans and policies aimed at improving LTC services. ADB can help developing member countries (DMCs) to invest in policies and programs that promote healthy aging and allow older persons to participate fully in society, including in the labor market, until an advanced age. This can also help reduce the burdens and costs for governments of LTC services.

Thailand is one of six DMCs participating in this project. The other countries are Indonesia, Mongolia, Sri Lanka, Tonga, and Viet Nam. In collaboration with the participating DMCs and centers of excellence, the project aims to (i) build a knowledge base in the region on the development of LTC systems and services, and identify potential investments in selected countries; (ii) develop the capacity of DMC officials and other stakeholders in strategic planning for the implementation of LTC across multiple sectors (e.g., health, social protection, urban development, transport); and (iii) create a knowledge network for disseminating good practices and expertise.

This country diagnostic study aims to provide a knowledge base comprising some basic facts about LTC in Thailand—specifically, emerging LTC policies, institutional arrangements, and stakeholder mapping; service provision, including existing programs and coverage; human resources and training programs; quality management, standards, and assessments; and financing.

1.1 Definition of Long-Term Care: International and National

The *World Report on Ageing and Health,* published by the World Health Organization (WHO), defines LTC as follows: "the activities undertaken by others to ensure that people with or at risk of a significant ongoing loss of intrinsic capacity can maintain a level of functional ability consistent with their basic rights, fundamental freedoms and human dignity."[2]

In Thailand, the Second National Health Assembly, held on 18 December 2009, endorsed Resolution 11 on the development of an LTC system for dependent older persons (aged 60 and above), and defined LTC for older persons as follows:

---

[2]   WHO. 2015. *World Report on Ageing and Health.* Geneva. p. 127.

Figure 1: Conceptual Framework of Long-Term Care in Thailand

Other services and measures

Community-based LTC

Volunteer

Family

More disabilities
No caregivers

Multimorbidity

Fragility

Dependency

Living at home

Institutional LTC

Aging

Environment modification
Health literacy
Health promotion

Active

Active Aging

LTC = long-term care.

Note: Other services and policies include health-care and social protection measures such as the old-age allowance, disability allowances, and welfare benefits.

Source: Illustration by authors.

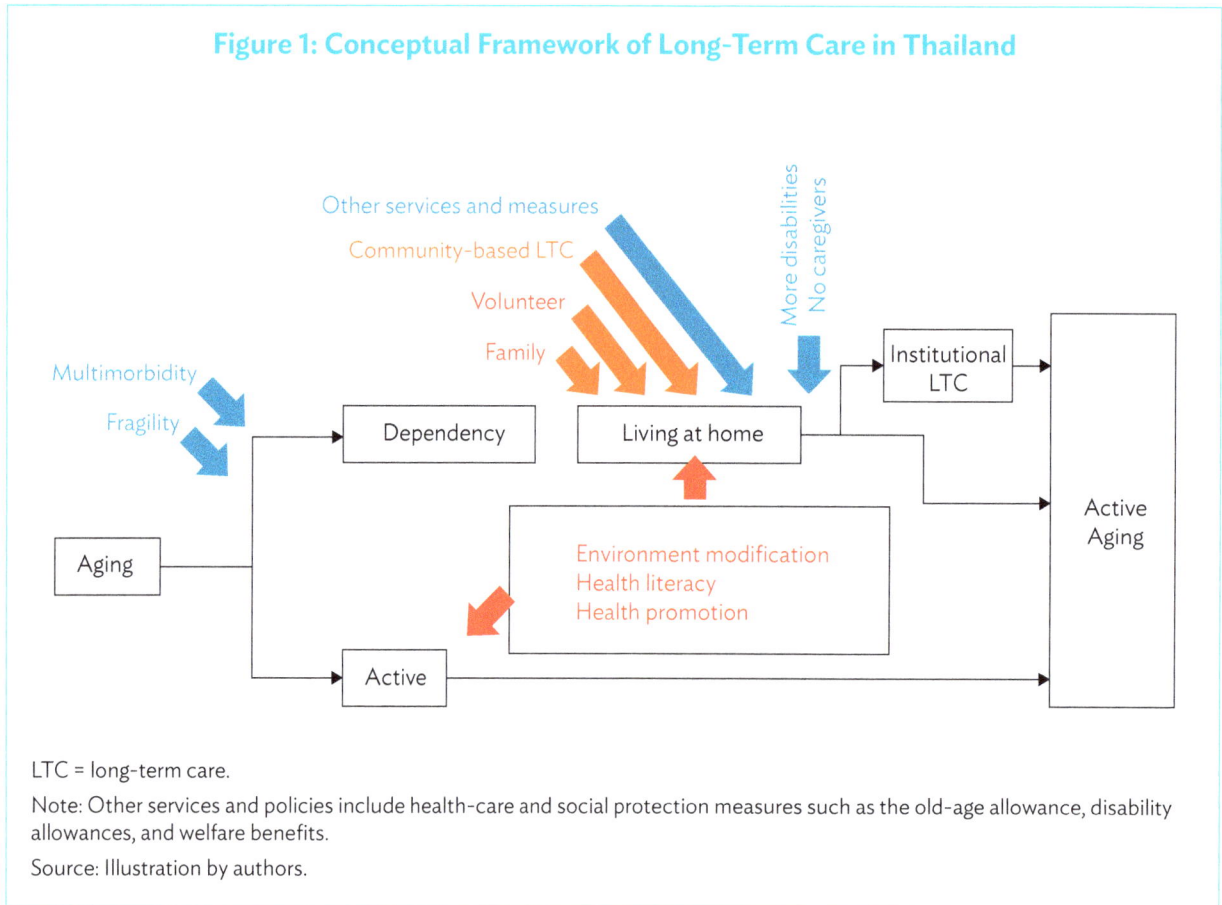

LTC for older persons refers to all dimensions of care, including social, health, economic, and environmental aspects. Older persons who have difficulties due to chronic disease or disability and are partially or totally dependent on others for daily living activities need LTC. It is provided by formal care personnel (professionals in health and social work) and informal caregivers (family members, friends, and neighbors) and may include care services provided by the family, community, or institution.[3]

Both the WHO and Thai definitions of LTC are rather broad, but the Thai definition does specify who needs care, the settings in which care occurs, and the types of care provided.

Thailand's framework for LTC is based on the concept of active aging. For older persons with a degree of dependency, aging in place remains the priority, and care services and other measures are either already in place or being developed. Residential nursing LTC is intended for those with complex care needs and with insufficient caregiving support at home (Figure 1).

---

[3] National Health Commission Office (NHCO): Thailand, Second National Health Assembly. 2009. *Development of Long-term Care for Dependent Elderly People.* Nonthaburi, Thailand: NHCO.

1.2 Country Context

Thailand is an aging society. **In 2017, older persons made up approximately 11 million, or 16.7%, of the total population**.[4] The proportion of older persons aged 60 and above who were women was 55%, and of those aged 80 and above, 61% (footnote 3). While more than 90% of the population is ethnically Thai, there are a number of ethnic minority groups. Most Thai people are Buddhists (94.2%), followed by Muslims (4.6%), and then those of other religions. There are around 3.5 million–4.0 million foreigners living in Thailand, the majority of whom are irregular migrants from Thailand's three neighboring countries: Cambodia, the Lao People's Democratic Republic, and Myanmar.[5] As a result of the Government of Thailand's immigration policies, there has been an increase in the number of foreigners—including those from Japan, the Republic of Korea, and the Russian Federation—who are residing in Thailand on retirement visas, and who may also require care services. See other basic country statistics in Table 1.

The Kingdom of Thailand is located in continental Southeast Asia, occupying an area of 513,115 square kilometers. The Central Thailand region comprises mainly lowland plains, with highlands concentrated in the Northeastern region and mountains located in the regions of Northern Thailand and Southern Thailand. The country is divided into 76 provinces. Ministerial functions are delegated to the provincial level under the supervision of provincial governors, who are civil servants. The governors work with the assigned officials from central administrative agencies. Local administrations currently have a limited role, although there are plans to further decentralize responsibilities by increasing the administrative powers of the local authorities.

The recent Thai socioeconomic situation has affected economic growth, slowing it down to 2.5% in 2019.[6] Future growth is projected to remain low (3%–5%) due to structural challenges, low productivity, and the aging society.[7] Poverty and inequality are continuing challenges for Thailand, with 9.9% of the population (6.7 million) classified as poor in 2018 (footnote 5).[8] Among older persons, 86% receive monetary and nonmonetary support from their children (footnote 3). However, older persons' direct income from other sources is increasing, for example, from pensions.

---

[4]   Government of Thailand, National Statistical Office (NSO). 2018. *Report on the 2017 Survey of the Older Persons in Thailand* [in Thai]. Bangkok.

[5]   J.W. Huguet, ed. 2014. *Thailand Migrant Report 2014*. Bangkok: United Nations Thematic Working Group on Migration in Thailand.

[6]   World Bank Group. 2020. *Thailand Economic Monitor, January 2020: Productivity for Prosperity*. Bangkok: World Bank; and J. Yang, S. Wang, B. Hansl, S. Zaidi, and P.K. Milne. 2020. *Taking the Pulse of Poverty and Inequality in Thailand*. Washington, DC: World Bank.

[7]   S. Jitsuchon. 2012. Thailand in a Middle-Income Trap. *TDRI Quarterly Review*. 27 (2). pp. 13–20; S. Jitsuchon. 2014. *Stability Growth: Fiscal Rules and Good Governance*. Paper presented at the Thailand Development Research Institute (TDRI) Annual Conference 2014: Positioning Thailand in the Next Three Decades; Four Challenges to Quality Growth. Bangkok. 22 November; Thailand Development Research Center. 2015. *Revenue Sources for Thai Health Care System: Macroeconomic Perspective; Analysis and Synthesis of Academic Work for Sustainable Financing Health System in Thailand* [in Thai]. Bangkok; and Government of Thailand, Ministry of Public Health (MOPH), Subcommittee on the Deployment and Reform of the Health System for Health Financing and Social Health Protection. 2016. *Report on the Deployment and Reform of the Health System for Health Financing and Social Health Protection: Phase 2*. Nonthaburi, Thailand.

[8]   In 2018, the poverty rate based on the national poverty line was 9.85%; and the poverty rate in terms of purchasing power parity (PPP), at $3.20 a day, was 0.5%.

Table 1: Basic Statistics

Item	Statistics	Year	Source
Population	69,625,582	2019	Ministry of Interior
Male (% of total population)	48.7		
Female (% of total population)	51.3		
Total fertility rate (per woman)	1.51	2019	WPP 2019 (UN)
Infant mortality rate (per 1,000 live births)	7.0	2019	WPP 2019 (UN)
Mortality rate, under 5 (per 1,000 live births)	9.0	2019	WPP 2019 (UN)
Life expectancy at birth (years)	77	2019	WPP 2019 (UN)
Life expectancy at 60 (years)	22	2013	WPP 2019 (UN)
Age dependency ratio (% of working-age population)	41.9	2019	WPP 2019 (UN)
Age dependency ratio, old (% of working-age population)	18.4	2019	
Age dependency ratio, young (% of working-age population)	23.5	2019	
Rural population (% of total population)	50.0	2018	WDI (World Bank)
Labor force participation rate, total (% of total population aged 15 and above)	67.8	2018	WDI (World Bank) (national estimate)
Labor force participation rate, female (% of females working)	59.5	2018	
Labor force participation rate, male (% of males working)	76.5	2018	
GDP per capita (current $)	7,274	2018	WDI (World Bank)
• PPP (current international $)	19,051	2018	
• Current (local currency)	235,010	2018	
• Constant (local currency)	153,535	2018	
GINI index (World Bank estimate)	36.4	2018	WDI (World Bank)
Poverty headcount ratio at national poverty lines (% of population)	9.9	2018	WDI (World Bank)
Poverty headcount ratio at $3.20 a day (2011 PPP) (% of population)	0.5	2018	WDI (World Bank)
Poverty headcount ratio at $5.50 a day (2011 PPP) (% of population)	8.6	2018	WDI (World Bank)

GDP = gross domestic product, PPP = purchasing power parity, WDI = World Development Indicators, WPP = World Population Prospects, UN = United Nations.

Sources: United Nations, Department of Economic and Social Affairs. Population Dynamics: World Population Prospects 2019. https://population.un.org/wpp/ (accessed 9 April 2020); and World Bank. World Development Indicators. https://databank.worldbank.org/source/world-development-indicators (accessed 9 April 2020).

II. METHODS

Research for this project comprised desk research and a literature review of secondary sources focusing on LTC in Thailand. The literature review included national policy and planning documents, academic and research articles, annual reports, published papers, and relevant unpublished gray literature (Figure 2).

The literature search used PubMed and Google Scholar. The search criteria included qualitative or quantitative studies published in English and Thai, studies on populations of Thai adults aged over 60, and studies dating no earlier than 2013. The search terms used were "elderly," "aging," "old people," "older persons," "dependency," "long-term care," "institutional care," "residential care," and "aging policies."

We identified the gray literature from among studies and reports of research institutes and relevant government agencies, including the National Health Security Office (NHSO); National Economic and Social Development Board (NESDB), renamed the National Economic and Social Development Council; Ministry of Public Health (MOPH); Ministry of Social Development and Human Security (MSDHS); Thailand Development Research Institute; Health Insurance System Research Office (HISRO); the Health Systems Research Institute of Thailand; the Foundation of Thai Gerontology Research and Development Institute College of Population Studies, Chulalongkorn University; and the Institute for Population and Social Research. We also identified and included existing data, models, and analyses relating to LTC in Thailand.

An exercise to map stakeholders relevant to LTC, including line ministries and other national, regional, and local institutions, identified key informants and individuals to include in consultations and interviews. We invited the identified informants to an initial consultation to gain information on the current situation and emerging trends regarding LTC systems, services, and investment. The consultation attendees included representatives from the Ministry of Finance (MOF), fiscal policy analysts, economists, actuaries, and people working in social-welfare elderly-care systems and services. We also conducted in-depth interviews (about knowledge, attitudes, beliefs, and practices) with stakeholders, including members of Parliament.

After identifying the initial gaps, we verified the analysis through a consultative meeting with core organizations, and presented this information to the deputy minister of finance. Then we produced an initial gap analysis report that incorporated comments from the participants and from the MOF.

This report has also formed the basis of discussion for a focus group of key stakeholders from the MOF; Department of Health Service Support (DHSS), under the MOPH; the NHSO; Office of Insurance Commission (OIC); Faculty of Medicine, Ramathibodi Hospital; Department of Statistics, Chulalongkorn Business School; and the Thai Elderly Promotion and Health Care Association (TEPHA). The focus group further verified the findings and discussed key issues that were incorporated into the draft study report.

The draft report was shared with the Asian Development Bank (ADB), and then a national consultation with stakeholders was organized. Comments from the consultative meeting were also integrated into the final report.

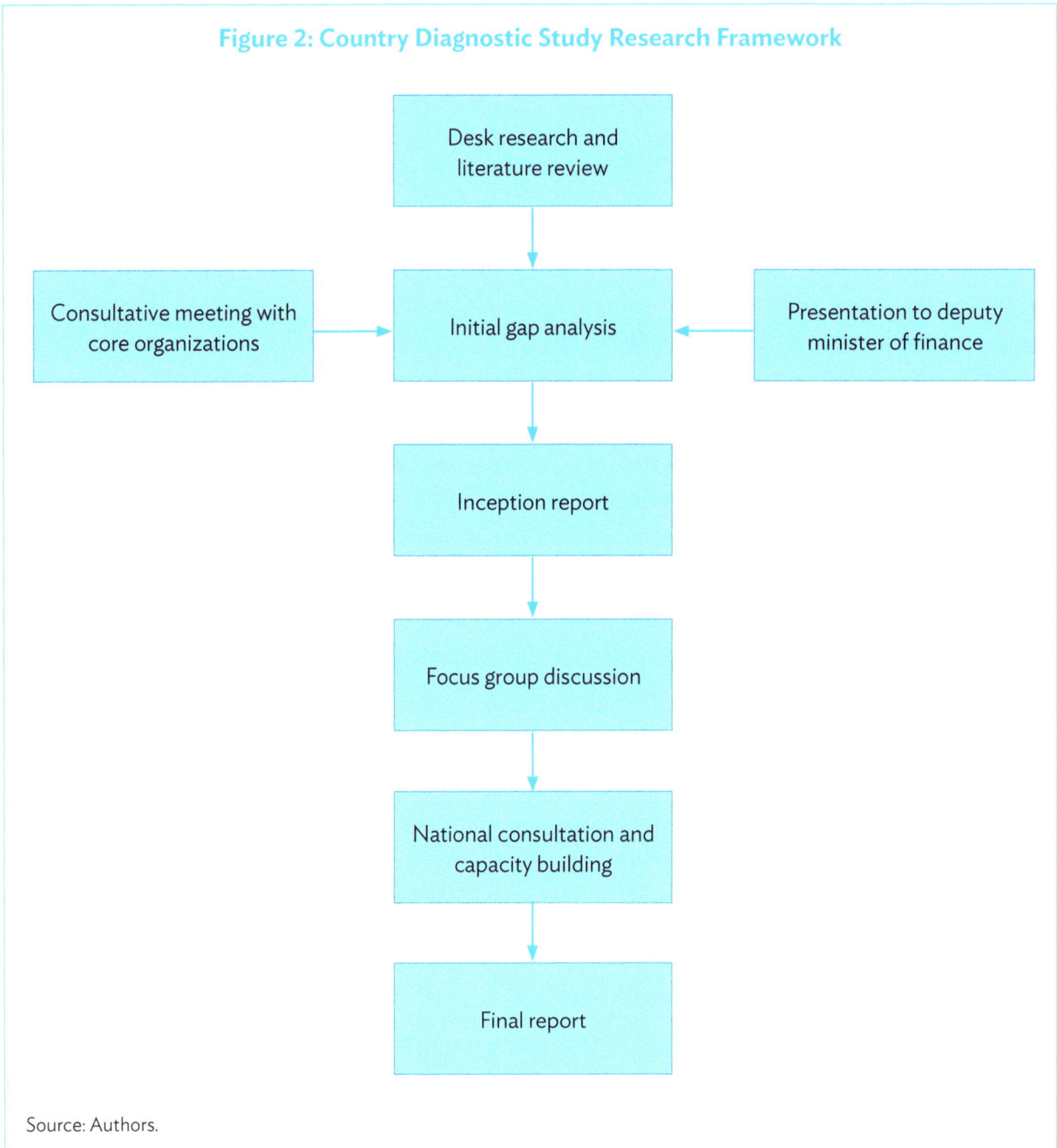

Figure 2: Country Diagnostic Study Research Framework

```
                    ┌─────────────────────┐
                    │  Desk research and  │
                    │  literature review  │
                    └──────────┬──────────┘
                               │
                               ▼
┌──────────────────┐  ┌─────────────────────┐  ┌──────────────────────┐
│ Consultative     │  │                     │  │ Presentation to      │
│ meeting with     │─▶│  Initial gap        │◀─│ deputy minister of   │
│ core             │  │  analysis           │  │ finance              │
│ organizations    │  │                     │  │                      │
└──────────────────┘  └──────────┬──────────┘  └──────────────────────┘
                               │
                               ▼
                    ┌─────────────────────┐
                    │  Inception report   │
                    └──────────┬──────────┘
                               │
                               ▼
                    ┌─────────────────────┐
                    │ Focus group         │
                    │ discussion          │
                    └──────────┬──────────┘
                               │
                               ▼
                    ┌─────────────────────┐
                    │ National            │
                    │ consultation and    │
                    │ capacity building   │
                    └──────────┬──────────┘
                               │
                               ▼
                    ┌─────────────────────┐
                    │   Final report      │
                    └─────────────────────┘
```

Source: Authors.

III. FINDINGS

3.1 Understanding Thailand's Care Needs

3.1.1 Demography

According to statistics from the Ministry of Interior, the Thai population was 69,625,582 in 2019, of which 48.7% were male and 51.3% were female. The population density in Thailand was 135 people per square kilometer.[9] Thailand is an aging society. The population age structure pyramid is changing shape due to the decreased total fertility rate and increased life expectancy (Figure 3).

The total fertility rate was 1.51 in 2019 and could decrease to 1.30 by 2040.[10] Factors influencing the low fertility rate include individuals staying single, delayed marriage, family planning, the financial burden of having more children, and the impact of childbearing on career development and the urban lifestyle.[11]

Life expectancy at birth was 73.12 years for men and 80.62 years for women in 2019.[12] The National Economic and Social Development Council forecasts that, by 2040, life expectancy at birth will increase to 75.25 years for men and 81.86 years for women. Life expectancy at 60 is predicted to be 20.20 years for men and 23.60 years for women; and life expectancy at 65 is anticipated to be 16.50 for men and 19.50 years for women.[13]

The number of older persons is expected to increase from 11.3 million (16.7% of the Thai population) in 2017 to 22.9 million (33% of the Thai population) by 2040.[14] The proportion of women will increase slightly, from 55% of older persons in 2010 to 57% by 2040. The total dependency ratio will increase from 41% in 2010 to 61% by 2040. The increasing number of older persons is significant for the dependency ratio. Age dependency ratios are projected to be 13% in 2010, 19% in 2020, 29% by 2030, and 40% by 2040 (Table 2).

---

[9] World Bank. 2017. *Population Density (People Per Sq. Km of Land Area)*. https://data.worldbank.org/indicator/EN.POP.DNST.

[10] Government of Thailand, Office of the National Economic and Social Development Board. 2013. *Population Projections for Thailand 2010–2040*. Bangkok.

[11] C. Peek, W. Im-em, and R. Tangthanaseth. 2016. *The State of Thailand's Population 2015: Features of Thai Families in the Era of Low Fertility and Longevity*. Bangkok: United Nations Population Fund (UNFPA), Thailand Country Office, and National Economic and Social Development Board.

[12] Life expectancy at birth is the average number of years a person could expect to live after birth.

[13] Life expectancy at 60 is the average age that a person who has reached 60 by a given year could expect to live to, and the life expectancy at 65 is the average age that a person who has reached 65 by a given year could expect to live to. Institute for Population and Social Research, Mahidol University. 2018. "Population of Thailand, 2018." *Mahidol Population Gazette* 27 (January 2020). http://www.ipsr.mahidol.ac.th/ipsr/Contents/Documents/Gazette/Gazette2020EN.pdf.

[14] Government of Thailand, National Statistical Office (NSO). 2018. *Report on the 2017 Survey of the Older Persons in Thailand* [in Thai]. Bangkok; and United Nations, Population Division. 2019 Revision of World Population Prospects. https://population.un.org/wpp/ (accessed 5 April 2020).

Figure 3: Thai Population Pyramid in 2010, 2020, 2030, and 2040

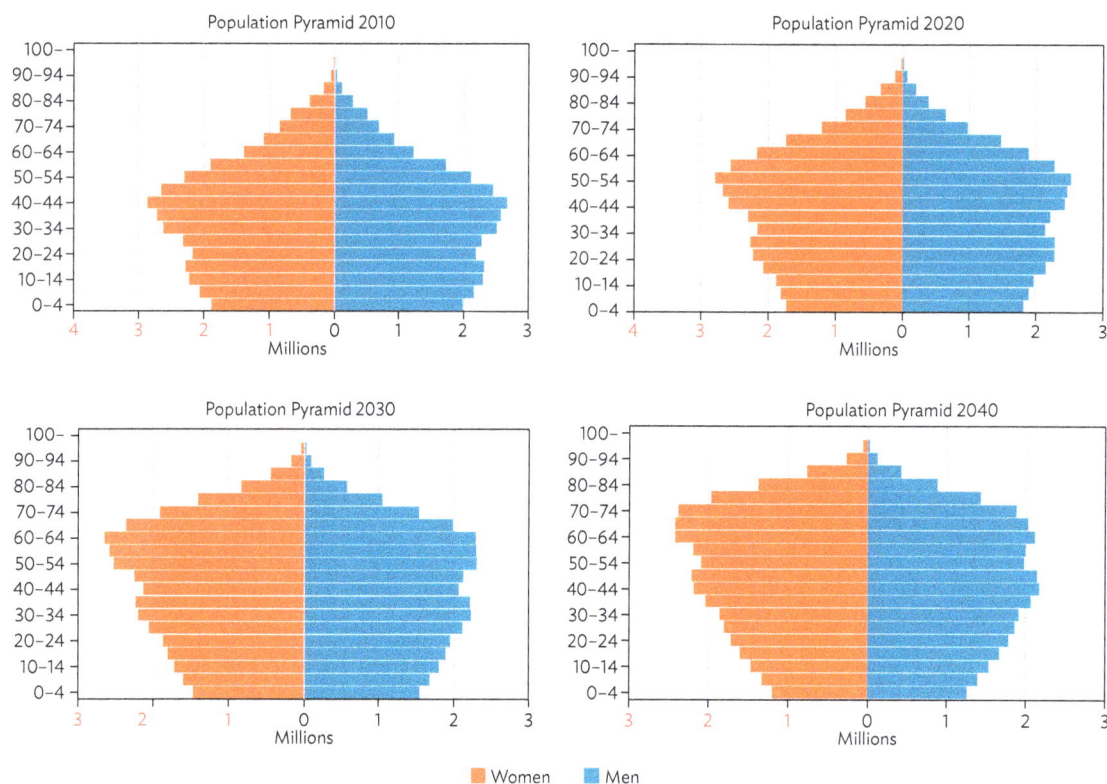

Source: Government of Thailand, Office of the National Economic and Social Development Board. 2011. Population Census 2010 and Population Projection. Bangkok.

Table 2: Proportions of Older Age Groups in the Overall Thai Population, 1990–2040
(per 1,000 people)

Age Groups	Female						Male					
	1990	2000	2010	2020	2030	2040	1990	2000	2010	2020	2030	2040
Total Population	27,501	30,901	32,705	35,834	36,306	35,716	27,031	30,015	31,084	33,966	34,040	33,292
60–69	1,282	1,873	2,469	4,092	5,292	5,224	1,175	1,628	2,160	3,532	4,506	4,459
Proportion 60–69 (%)	5	6	8	11	15	15	4	5	7	10	13	13
70–79	606	948	1,518	2,171	3,531	4,639	486	759	1,190	1,696	2,785	3,653
Proportion 70–79 (%)	2	3	5	6	10	13	2	3	4	5	8	11
80+	259	359	644	1,168	1,772	2,963	167	226	426	753	1,122	1,930
Proportion 80+ (%)	1	1	2	2	5	8	1	1	1	2	3	6

Sources: Government of Thailand, National Statistical Office. Population and Housing Census 1990, 2000, and 2010. http://web.nso.go.th/en/census/poph/cen_poph.htm (accessed 5 April 2020); and United Nations, Population Division. 2019 Revision of World Population Prospects. https://population.un.org/wpp/ (accessed 5 April 2020).

3.1.2   Thailand's Progress in Calculating the Need for Care

Since 2008, four different estimates of Thailand's need for LTC have been calculated, each using different approaches. These are presented to give as complete an understanding of the issue as possible.

In 2008, the first estimate forecast that people over 60 with severe dependency would comprise 1.4%–1.9% of the male population and 1.7%–2.0% of the female population (2004–2024).[15]

The second estimate, published in 2013, drew data from two sources to estimate disability prevalence.[16] One was a study of an LTC system for the protection of older persons and the other was the Fourth National Health Examination Survey (2008–2009).[17] Both surveys used the Barthel Index, which measures activities of daily living (ADL).[18] In both sources, the data were aggregated into four levels: ADL scores of 0–40, which reflected severe disability; ADL scores of 41–74, which reflected moderate disability; ADL scores of 75–90, which reflected mild disability; and ADL scores of more than 90, which were classified as independent.

Table 3: Prevalence of Disability by Level of Severity
(%)

Age Group	Severe	Moderate	Mild
60–69	0.80	0.50	1.69
70–79	2.62	1.49	3.86
80+	10.54	3.06	8.16

Source: O. Prasitsiriphon et al. 2013. *Costing Model for Long-Term Care System in Thailand.* Bangkok: Health System Research Office.

The prevalence of disability by level of severity and sex is used to project the number of older persons with disabilities in the future. The prevalence rate is assumed to remain constant during the projection period. The numbers of dependent people in each cohort (i.e., age group) are calculated using the prevalence rate of disability. Then the dependents in each cohort are disaggregated into four groups based on their level of disability using the Barthel Index. The prevalence of disability increases as people age (Table 3).

Table 5 reflects data from the third estimate, published in the *Report on the 2017 Survey of the Older Persons in Thailand* (2018). The survey posed questions about four functional limitations, eight ADL, and three instrumental activities of daily living (IADL). Among the respondents, **35% reported some limitation in at least one functional-limitation domain, 28% in one or more IADL, and 7% in one or more ADL.** Only 8% reported

---

[15]   S. Srithamrongsawat et al. 2009. *Projection of Demand and Expenditure for Institutional Long Term Care in Thailand.* Bangkok: Health Insurance System Research Office.

[16]   O. Prasitsiriphon et al. 2013. *Costing Model for Long-Term Care System in Thailand.* Bangkok: Health System Research Office.

[17]   W. Suwanrada, S. Sasat, and S. Kumruangrit. 2010. Demand for Long-Term Care Service for Older Persons in Bangkok. *Journal of Economic and Public Policy.* 1 (1). pp. 20–41; and W. Aekplakorn. 2009. *Report on the Fourth National Health Examination Survey: 2008–2009.* Bangkok: National Health Security Office.

[18]   The Barthel Index comprises 10 items that measure a person's self-care abilities, including ADL and mobility. The items include grooming, bathing, feeding, transferring to and from a toilet, moving from a wheelchair to a bed and back again, walking on a level surface, going up and down stairs, dressing, and continence of bowels and bladder. The version that was used came from Collin et al. (1998), in which the total = 100 points.

Table 4: Numbers of People in Thailand Living with Dependency, 2010 and 2020

Level of Dependency	Age	2010	2020
Severe (male)	60–69	17,066	26,507
	70–79	40,223	54,706
	80+	27,859	42,536
	Total male	85,148	123,750
Severe (female)	60–69	19,755	31,202
	70–79	31,728	43,014
	80+	83,101	134,040
	Total female	134,585	208,255
Moderate (male)	60–69	11,449	17,783
	70–79	22,016	29,942
	80+	15,932	24,325
	Total male	49,397	72,051
Moderate (female)	60–69	11,853	18,721
	70–79	19,128	25,932
	80+	17,329	27,951
	Total female	48,310	72,604
Mild (male)	60–69	34,132	53,015
	70–79	25,586	34,798
	80+	7,966	12,163
	Total male	67,683	99,975
Mild (female)	60–69	43,462	68,644
	70–79	76,208	103,315
	80+	76,208	122,922
	Total female	195,878	294,881

Note: The numbers for 2020 are estimates.

Source: O. Prasitsiriphon et al. 2014. *Costing Model for Long-Term Care System in Thailand*. Bangkok: Health System Research Office.

requiring assistance to overcome their limitations. Also, older age is associated with increased difficulties with both ADL and IADL, for which competency is essential for leading an independent life. In the survey, 7.6% of older persons reported having difficulty with at least one ADL, while 24.6% reported having difficulty with at least one IADL.

Findings from the survey confirmed that limitations increase with age: about 20% of those aged 60–64 were experiencing difficulties in at least one domain, but that was true for almost 75% of those aged 80 and above. It also found that 45% of older women were experiencing difficulties, compared with about 30% of older men. Among rural populations, there was a slight increase in the prevalence of limitations compared with urban

Table 5: Percentages of the Older Population with Functional or Daily Living Difficulties, by Age, Gender, and Area of Residence, 2017

Type of Difficulty	Total	Age			Gender		Type of Area	
		60–69	70–79	80+	Men	Women	Urban	Rural
Functional Difficulties								
Lifting 5 kilograms	28.6	15.9	38.6	67.2	20.0	36.0	29.1	28.2
Squatting	19.1	10.0	25.0	46.8	14.0	23.4	20.0	18.6
Walking 200–300 meters	15.7	6.6	20.3	46.4	11.2	19.5	14.7	16.4
Climbing two or three stairs	14.3	6.0	17.9	43.4	10.3	17.5	13.7	14.7
Any functional difficulty	33.4	19.8	45.5	73.9	24.4	41.3	34.1	33.0
Difficulties with ADL								
Getting up from lying down	5.4	2.3	5.8	17.3	4.4	6.2	5.8	5.1
Using toilet	4.0	1.5	3.7	15.5	3.2	4.7	4.2	3.9
Bathing	3.8	1.5	3.3	15.0	3.1	4.4	4.2	3.6
Dressing	3.4	1.4	2.9	12.7	2.8	3.8	3.7	3.1
Washing face and brushing teeth	2.7	1.1	2.4	9.9	2.1	3.1	2.7	2.6
Putting on shoes	3.2	1.4	2.8	11.9	2.8	3.6	3.4	3.1
Grooming self	2.9	1.3	2.6	10.4	2.7	3.1	3.0	2.8
Eating	2.8	1.1	2.7	10.0	2.3	3.2	2.9	2.8
Any ADL difficulty	7.6	3.4	7.9	24.5	6.3	8.6	7.8	7.4
Difficulties with IADL								
Taking bus or boat on own	23.4	9.9	33.0	67.9	16.7	29.2	21.6	24.7
Counting change	7.2	2.5	8.3	25.5	5.7	8.4	6.2	7.9
Taking medicines	8.7	2.9	9.8	31.2	6.9	10.2	7.9	9.3
Any IADL difficulty	24.6	10.9	35.0	69.3	17.8	30.4	22.4	26.2
Any functional, ADL or IADL difficulty listed above	36.8	22.4	51.4	79.8	27.6	45.0	36.0	37.4

ADL = activities of daily living, IADL = instrumental activities of daily living.
Source: Government of Thailand, National Statistical Office. 2018. *Report on the 2017 Survey of the Older Persons in Thailand* [in Thai]. Bangkok.

populations, and while difficulty with just one functional domain, ADL, or IADL is common, over one-third of those with difficulties experienced limitations across all domains.

The fourth estimate resulted from the Fifth National Health Examination Survey (NHES V), conducted in 2013–2014, which showed a higher prevalence of dependency among older persons in Thailand compared with NHES IV, conducted in 2007–2008.[19] A multistage sampling frame based on government registers was used. The total sample of older individuals (60 years old and above) was 7,365. The rate of older persons who needed help with two or more ADL or who were unable to perform continence-related tasks was 20.7% (16.6% of men and

[19] W. Aekplakorn. 2009. *Report on the Fourth National Health Examination Survey: 2008–2009.* Bangkok: National Health Security Office.

24.1% of women), compared with earlier rate of 15.5% (12.7% of men, 17.8% of women). This might be due to an increase in morbidity. The NHES V also found that 11.4% of respondents had limitations in one ADL, 10.4% had limitations in two ADL, and 4.1% had limitations in three ADL.

3.1.3   The Situation of Older Persons

When the current generation of older persons was young, Thailand was undergoing a period of rapid changes. One area of change was education. More than 85% of people over the age of 60 are either totally uneducated or have only a primary school education. However, younger old people (aged 60–80) are far more likely to have received an education than oldest-old people (aged 80 and above). In the future, a greater proportion of older persons will be better educated (footnote 3). Another area of change was health care. Older persons in Thailand had poorer access to health care as children than did the younger cohorts.

3.1.3.1   Living Arrangements

Older persons in Thailand usually live with one or more adult children, usually a daughter. However, the living arrangements of older persons are changing: coresidence with children has steadily declined since the mid-1990s, while the proportion of those living alone or with only the spouse has increased. Despite these changes, however, over half of older persons (55%) still live with a child and almost two-thirds (65%) either live with a child or adjacent to a child's home; only 9% of older persons live alone. Roughly 30% of older persons living alone or with only the spouse have a child living next door, and 46% have a child living within the locality (footnote 3). The majority of older men are married, but about half of older women are widowed. For those over the age of 80, the disparity is greater, with only 18% of women married, compared with over 60% of men. Household size has declined steadily, from just over 5 in 1986 to 3.6 in 2014. Older persons with fewer children are less likely to live with an adult child, suggesting that the trend toward smaller families, combined with the greater dispersion of children, will contribute to a continuing decline of coresidence with children.

3.1.3.2   Income

Among older persons with living children, 85% receive monetary and nonmonetary support from their children. In 2017, about 41% of older persons reported that their main source of income was their children, spouse, or relatives. The old-age allowance was the main source of income for 20% of older persons.[20] The percentage of older persons reporting private pensions as an income source remained quite low, at just 6%. Work was the main source of income for 31% of older persons (footnote 3). In 2018, one in three older persons in Thailand (4.4 million) was still working.[21] Older men were more likely to work than older women, with 59% of them working in the agriculture and fishery sectors. Nevertheless, the percentage of those still working declined steadily after the age of 64.

Self-assessed income adequacy improved across three surveys from 2007 to 2014. In 2014, 64% of older persons believed that their income was adequate or better. However, 36% of older persons reported either that their income was only sometimes adequate or that it was inadequate (Figure 4). The main source of income bears a direct relationship to the assessment of income adequacy. Older persons whose main income was their old-age allowance usually assessed their situation least favorably. Respondents aged over 70, women, and rural older persons were more likely to consider their income to be inadequate (footnote 3).

---

[20]   Section 9 (5) of the Act on the Elderly B.E (Buddhist Era) 2545 (2003 A.D.), regarding the old-age allowance, was revised in a second version of the act in B.E. 2553 (2010).

[21]   Foundation of Thai Gerontology Research and Development Institute (TGRI). 2019. *Situation of the Thai Elderly 2018.* Bangkok.

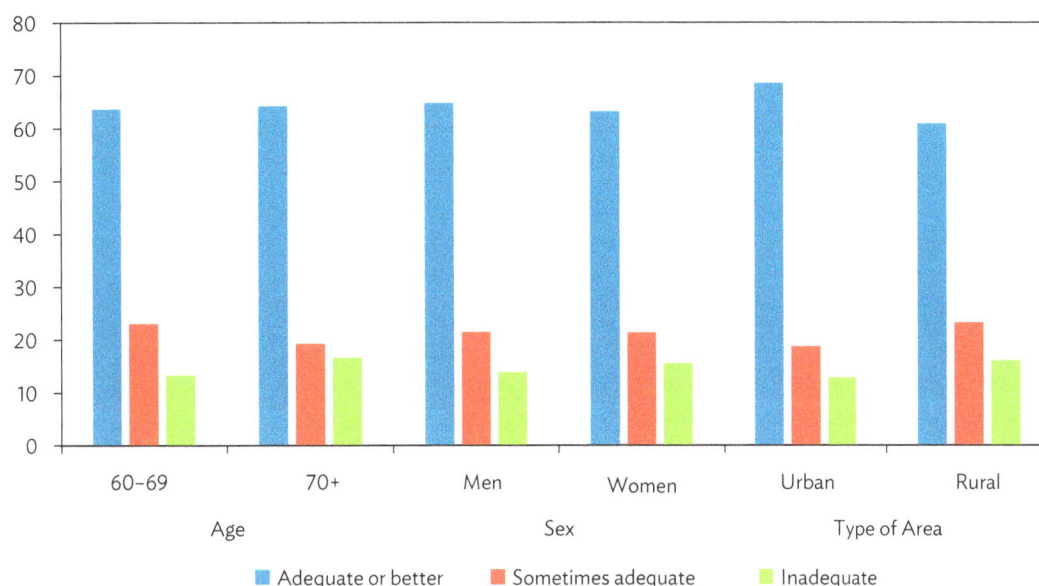

Figure 4: Self-Assessed Adequacy of Income, 2014
(%)

Source: J. Knodel et al. 2015. The Situation of Thailand's Older Population: An Update Based on the 2014 Survey of Older Persons in Thailand. *Research Collection School of Social Sciences.* Paper 1948. Singapore: Singapore Management University.

3.1.4   Health and Disability

According to World Health Statistics 2019, **the healthy life expectancy at birth in Thailand was 64.0 years for men and 69.8 years for women in 2016.**[22]

According to the 2017 Survey of the Older Persons in Thailand, 53% of older Thai people reported that they had at least one chronic disease (footnote 3). The Fifth National Health Examination Survey (NHES V) confirmed that there was a higher prevalence of obesity,[23] diabetes mellitus, and hypertension, compared with the 2007–2008 survey (NHES IV). Specifically, the prevalence of obesity among people aged 60–69 in 2017 was 41.4%, among those aged 70–79, 32.1%, and among those aged 80 and over, 17.6%; the prevalence of diabetes mellitus among people aged 60–69 was 19.2%, among those aged 70–79, 18.8%, and among those aged 80 and over, 11.8%; and the prevalence of hypertension among those aged 60–69 was 48.4%, among those aged 70–79, 56.8%, and among those aged 80 and over, 64.9%.[24] The self-assessed health status for those aged 60+ was *very good, good,* or *fair* for 84% of the respondents. The remaining 16% reported their health status as *poor* or *very poor.* Self-reporting as poor or very poor health increases with age, from 9% of those aged 60–64 to 33% of those aged over 80. Only 11.1% of older persons recalled falling ill in the previous 6 months (footnote 3).

---

[22]   WHO. 2019. *World Health Statistics 2019: Monitoring Health for the SDGs, Sustainable Development Goals.* Geneva.

[23]   A person is considered overweight when his or her body mass index, or BMI, is equal to or above 25, and obese when the BMI is equal to or greater than 30. The BMI is a person's weight in kilograms divided by the square of his or her height in meters.

[24]   W. Aekplakorn. 2014. *Report on the Fifth National Health Examination Survey: 2013–2014.* Nonthaburi, Thailand: National Health Examination Security Office.

The 2017 Survey of the Older Persons in Thailand, conducted by the National Statistical Office (NSO), found that **around 7% of older persons had experienced falls during the prior 6 months** (footnote 3).

As many as 51% of older persons reported clear vision without eyeglasses, and an additional 33% reported clear vision with eyeglasses. Access to eyeglasses and/or surgery seems to have increased significantly since 2007, as the reporting of unclear vision dropped from 21% in 2007 to 15% in 2017. This trend was attributable to the greater availability of vision screening, eyeglasses, and surgery for rural older persons (footnote 3).

About 15% of older persons had difficulty with hearing. Of these, only 0.3% were considered deaf, and 2.4% were able to hear clearly with the use of their hearing aids. Difficulties with incontinence was also a significant issue; it increased with age, affecting 7.1% of those aged 60–69, and up to about 41.6% of those aged 80 and above (footnote 3).

The rate of disability increases among older persons. The overall disability rate in Thailand is 2.2%, of which more than 57% are over the age of 60. Of all the people over 60, 16.8% have a disability.[25] It may be useful for Thailand to standardize the classifications of disabilities and functional limitations, particularly with regard to older persons. This is because many older persons, despite functional limitations, do not consider themselves to be suffering from a disability.

3.1.5   Demand for Care

Due to the comprehensive benefits package of universal health coverage and health services, **the prevalence of unmet needs for outpatient services for all ages is 1.4%, and for inpatient services, 0.4%.**[26] This assessment of unmet needs was studied using a standard set of Organisation for Economic Co-operation and Development (OECD) unmet need questionnaires in the fourth wave of the Panel Socio-Economic Survey (Panel SES), conducted in 2010 by the NSO. Although the prevalence of unmet needs was low, at under 3% across all categories, indicating the considerable success of universal coverage, the unmet needs for outpatient and inpatient services were significantly higher for rural dwellers than for urban dwellers, for those in lower-income quintiles than for those in higher-income quintiles, and for older persons than for children and younger adults.

Table 6, reproduced from the NSO's *Report on the 2017 Survey of the Older Persons in Thailand* (2018), shows those who reported needing or desiring care assistance with ADL, the main indicator for long-term care (LTC) demand, and the actual assistance provided. **The data shows a total demand for care among those over the age of 60 at 8.3%, with 25.5% of those aged 80+ reporting a need or desire for assistance.** Of those who reported a need or desire for assistance, 33.9% were not receiving any. Interestingly, the proportion of unmet care needs was higher for younger age groups. This may indicate that, for older persons, families are more responsive to meeting care needs. It also highlights the need for interventions or care assistance to be available at the earlier stages of functional decline.

There is a strong preference among older Thai people to remain in their homes, rather than move to an LTC residential care facility. A survey of the demand for LTC in Bangkok found that 90% of older persons were unwilling to stay in an LTC residential care facility, and the main reasons why included the belief that care from family members is better, a lack of funds, an unwillingness to spend money on residential care, and a lack of trust

[25]   United Nations Economic and Social Commission for Asia and the Pacific (ESCAP). 2016. *Disability at a Glance 2015: Strengthening Employment Prospects for Persons with Disabilities in Asia and the Pacific.* Bangkok.

[26]   N. Thammatacharee et al. 2012. Prevalence and Profiles of Unmet Healthcare Need in Thailand. *BMC Public Health.* 12. p. 923.

Table 6: Persons Over 60 Needing/Desiring Assistance with Daily Living Activities and Percentage Receiving It, by Age, Gender, and Area of Residence, 2017
(%)

Category	Among All		Among Those Reporting a Need/Desire for Assistance		Among Those Reporting No Need/Desire for Assistance	
	Reporting Need or Desire for Assistance	Reporting Receiving Assistance	Receiving Assistance	Not Receiving Assistance	Receiving Assistance	Not Receiving Assistance
By Age						
60–64	3.9	7.6	43.3	56.7	6.2	93.8
65–69	4.9	8.8	46.0	54.0	6.9	93.1
70–74	7.7	14.3	61.8	38.2	10.3	89.7
75–79	8.9	16.0	60.5	39.5	11.6	88.4
80+	25.5	36.5	84.8	15.2	20.1	79.9
By Gender						
Men	7.0	12.6	63.3	36.7	8.8	91.2
Women	9.4	15.2	67.8	32.2	9.7	90.3
By Area						
Urban	8.1	14.7	72.5	27.5	9.7	90.3
Rural	8.5	13.5	61.8	38.2	9.0	91.0
Total	8.3	14.0	66.1	33.9	9.3	90.7

Source: Government of Thailand, National Statistical Office (NSO). 2018. *Report on the 2017 Survey of the Older Persons in Thailand* [in Thai]. Bangkok.

in the quality of care at the residential facilities. Those willing to stay in a residential LTC facility cited the lack of a caregiver at home, the need for skilled assistance, and a desire to lessen the burden on the family.[27]

3.2 Supply of Care

The supply of care in Thailand can be formal or informal, paid or unpaid, at home or in residential facilities. Families provide most of the care given to older persons, at home and without payment. Home-based care provided by trained volunteers or paid caregivers is growing, and helps to support informal care-support systems. In particular, the Community-Based Long-Term Care Program, under the National Health Security Office (NHSO), started in 2016 and had provided care to some 193,000 older persons by 2018; there are plans to expand it throughout the country. Residential nursing care and specialist care are less available, but they are growing as well. The Ministry of Social Development and Human Security manages public homes called "Social Welfare Development Centers for Older Persons," which aim to provide shelter, but also a degree of care for residents if they develop care support needs.

---

[27] W. Suwanrada, S. Sasat, and S. Kumruangrit. 2010. Demand for Long-Term Care Service for Older Persons in Bangkok. *Journal of Economic and Public Policy.* 1 (1). pp. 20–41; and W. Suwanrada et al. 2010. *Long-Term Care System for Old-Age Security Promotion* [in Thai]. Bangkok: Ministry of Social Development and Human Security, Office of the Welfare Promotion Protection and Empowerment of Vulnerable Groups.

3.2.1 Care by Families

In Thailand, most elderly care by far is provided by families, with over 90% of people needing care receiving it from family members. Children account for 57% of caregivers, of which the large majority are daughters (41%). Spouses are the second most common caregivers (32%), most frequently cited as primary caregivers to people in their 60s and 70s, predominantly caring for husbands (footnote 3).

Internal migration is a critical demographic issue in Thailand. The proportion of people aged 15–24 employed in agriculture dropped from about 35% in 1987 to less than 10% in 2016. The number of skip-generation households, where there are no working-age adults present, has doubled since the 1990s, and these households are more common in rural areas. In 2013, there were more than 400,000 skip-generation families in Thailand, and the trend is expected to grow in the future, as more people of working age migrate to urban areas. More than half of skip-generation household heads are older than 60 (footnote 9). This situation leads to decreased availability of care for older persons who are left behind, and who often have to care for young children. The number of households where older persons (aged at least 60) live with working-age family members declined from 77% in 1986 to 52% in 2017 (footnote 3).

Although the supply of care from within families is declining, **there is a growing supply of available labor from neighboring countries.** It is estimated by the United Nations Thematic Working Group on Migration in Thailand, a task force led by the International Organization for Migration (IOM), that there are between 3.5 million and 4.0 million foreigners living in Thailand (footnote 4). About 2.7 million of them are from the neighboring countries of Cambodia, the Lao People's Democratic Republic, and Myanmar. Almost all of these people are low-skilled workers, some of whom perform domestic housework or care for older persons.

3.2.2 Supply of Formal Care

Formal care is provided by volunteers, professionals and nonprofessionals in the health and social sectors, and specific LTC service providers, both public and private. Table 7 presents the best estimates of the numbers of various types of formal care workers, although more reliable data would be needed to be certain of the figures. More details regarding the qualifications, roles, and certification for each category can be found in the section on human resources.

Government-sponsored volunteer groups play a significant role in responding to the care needs of older persons. Some of the volunteers counted in Table 7 may be double-counted, as there were 1 million "village health volunteers" (VHVs) in 2018 and most LTC "volunteer caregivers," as well as those working with Home Care Volunteers for the Elderly (HCVE), are also VHVs. It is also worth noting that the Friends Help Friends project is reported to be no longer operational.

Local authorities manage the HCVE scheme, a home-based care program with an emphasis on social care and referral services. There are over 80,000 HCVE volunteers, and they reach almost 800,000 older persons.

The NHSO's Community-Based Long-Term Care Program, piloted in 2016, trained 44,000 volunteers and paid caregivers in its first 3 years. These caregivers provide home care services mainly to bedbound and housebound older persons, including a relatively comprehensive package of services with health and social care elements. With a ratio of one caregiver to 7–10 dependent older persons, however, 130,000–185,714 caregivers would be needed to cover the 1.3 million dependent older persons that a full rollout of the program would target.

Table 7: Numbers of Volunteers and Professionals Caring for Older Persons, 2018

Formal Carers/Caregivers	Number
Volunteers	
Village health volunteers	1,067,746
Home Care Volunteers for the Elderly Program	80,000
Friends Help Friends project	8,074[a]
Volunteer caregivers	72,000
Professionals	
Medical doctors	36,938
Geriatricians	40
Geriatric nurses	...
Registered nurses	165,541
Technical nurses	7,257
Practical nurses	7,000
Physiotherapists	4,836
Occupational therapists	1,200
Social workers	...

... = data not available.

Notes: There are also several categories of paid nonprofessionals who care for older persons, including trained caregivers, care assistants, care teams, untrained paid caregivers, and domestic workers. However, no data are available regarding their numbers.

[a] This figure is from 2008.

Source: Government of Thailand, Ministry of Public Health. Number of Job Positions Classified by Year of Registration. http://www.thaiphc.net/phc/phcadmin/administrator/Report/OSMRP00012_2.php (accessed 5 April 2020).

Nongovernment organizations (NGOs) such as the Thai Red Cross Society, the Foundation for Older Persons' Development, the Duang Prateep Foundation, some religious organizations, and several other nonprofit organizations provide community care for older persons, especially those in poor and remote areas.

Residential care services for dependent older persons are found in private nursing homes, private hospitals, government residential homes, and homes for poor older persons supported by charitable organizations. These facilities provide services that include both basic and complex care, including accommodations, help with personal hygiene, assistance in ADL and transfers, care that requires nursing skills, rehabilitation, day care, respite care, and hospice care.[28] However, there are no data regarding the numbers of older persons receiving the various care services from these facilities.

The number of residential care facilities is increasing. A survey of residential LTC facilities for older persons (60 years and above) in Thailand by Sasat et al. (2009) found that there were 138 such institutions, of which

---

[28]   S. Sasat and T. Pukdeeprom. 2009. Nursing Home. *Journal of Population Studies.* 25 (1). pp. 45–62.

60 (43.48%) were private nursing homes and 44 (31.88%) were public not-for-profit residential homes. Of these institutions, 68 (49.28%) were located in Bangkok.[29] In 2016, the Department of Business Development, at the Ministry of Commerce (MOC), reported that there was a total of 442 nongovernment residential and nonresidential facilities providing care for older persons, of which two-thirds were private businesses and one-third were corporations.[30] Of these, there were 10 facilities run by non-Thai corporations. The number of private facilities found might be underrepresented by the report, however, as there are no specific laws or regulations on registration. Among those registered, facility owners were encouraged to join the Thai Elderly Promotion and Health Care Association (TEPHA). In 2016, TEPHA had only 110 members.

3.2.3   Care Ecosystem: Services from Other Sectors

3.2.3.1   Health Care

The health-care system in Thailand is an entrepreneurial system with public and private providers. Public health facilities have rapidly expanded nationwide since 1961. The facilities under the Ministry of Public Health (MOPH), comprising 9,768 health centers at the subdistrict level and 734 hospitals at the district level, are the main care providers, although there are also 17,671 private clinics, 322 private hospitals, and 11,154 private pharmacies.[31] Private hospitals are usually located in Bangkok and other urban areas. There are also many private clinics and polyclinics in urban areas, most of them owned and run by government-employed physicians working outside of their public-facility hours. The distribution of health personnel between urban and rural areas is a policy issue in Thailand. In 2001, the government launched its universal health scheme, which currently provides health insurance coverage to those without any other type of health insurance, such as the Social Security Scheme (SSS), which covers about 75% of the population.[32] Since 2001, the SSS has resulted in an increase in outpatient visits and hospital admissions, particularly among the poorer segments of the population. The program aims to increase access to and the affordability of its health-care services, with an emphasis on primary health. It is a tax-financed scheme with no copayments, and is managed by the NHSO, which also manages the HCVE.

There were about 1 million VHVs nationwide in 2018, working on advocacy for services and coordination in close connection with health-care personnel in communities. The VHVs were introduced by the MOPH in 1997. They play an important role in the public health system as change agents on the ground. Their work covers all age groups and their responsibilities include home visits to follow up on cases, data collection, health promotion, prevention supervision, basic health care and medication, rehabilitation, referrals, the organization of community activities to promote health development, and collaboration with community leaders and local administration organizations (LAOs)[33] to develop the public health systems in communities. On average, one VHV is responsible for 8–15 households, and there are about 10–20 VHVs per village. Welfare and benefits provided to the VHVs include a monthly allowance for transportation of B1,000 and discounted inpatient room charges. VHVs are more

---

[29]   S. Sasat et al. 2009. *Research Report on Long-Term Care Institutions in Thailand.* Nonthaburi, Thailand: Health Systems Research Institute of Thailand.

[30]   Government of Thailand, MOC, Department of Business Development. 2017. *Number of Establishments for Elderly Care.* Bangkok.

[31]   S. Srithamrongsawat. 2018. *Experience of Thailand LTC System Development.* Paper presented at the Indonesia National Workshop on LTC Strategy, organized by the Ministry of Planning and ADB. Jakarta. 25–27 April.

[32]   V. Schmitt, T. Sakunphanit, and O. Prasitsiriphol. 2013. *Social Protection Assessment Based National Dialogue: Towards a Nationally Defined Social Protection Floor in Thailand.* Bangkok: International Labour Organization (ILO) and the United Nations Country Team in Thailand.

[33]   In Thailand, there are four types of local administration organizations, namely, Provincial Administration Organizations (75); Municipalities, which include cities, towns, and subdistricts (2,410); and other types of local authorities as designated by laws, such as Bangkok Metropolitan Administration (1), Pattaya City (1), and nonmunicipal Subdistrict Administration Organizations (5,365).

effective in rural than in metropolitan areas. As VHVs cover all age groups and work on a voluntary basis, they can only provide care to older persons based on their capacity and availability.

3.2.3.2   Income Security and Pensions

Only civil servants and members of the SSS are able to receive pensions. However, the Act on the Elderly (2003) established an old-age allowance that every Thai person aged 60 or older, except government pensioners (former civil servants), can receive. The old-age allowance started as a means-tested allowance for poor older persons before changing into a universal pension scheme in 2009. Effective from October 2011, persons aged 60–69 receive a monthly allowance of B600, those aged 70–79 receive B700, those aged 80–89 receive B800, and those aged 90 or older receive B1,000. However, as the national poverty line is at B2,271 per month (B75.73 per day), the adequacy of the old-age allowance can be questioned. In addition to the old-age allowance, older Thai persons with a disability who have a disability identification card are eligible for the disability allowance, which is set at B800 per month, regardless of their economic status (footnote 20).

3.2.3.3   Financial Support

The Ministry of Social Development and Human Security (MSDHS) is responsible for arranging support for underprivileged older persons who are eligible for any of three categories of assistance specified by the ministry: (i) temporary financial assistance for older persons in danger of abuse, illegal exploitation, or abandonment (B500 per person); (ii) assistance in securing safe accommodations, food, and clothing up to three times a year for older persons with domestic problems (B2,000 per person); and (iii) support for older persons preparing traditional funerals (B2,000 per person).[34]

3.2.3.4   Age-Friendly Housing

"Age-friendly" refers to housing that is designed to meet the needs and lifestyles of older persons, and it is essential for enabling older persons to live independently for as long as possible and to prevent accidents. Similarly, to maximize older persons' productivity and safe participation in society, public spaces should maximize accessibility for them. Adaptations can be made in public transportation, roads, neighborhood design, and in the locations of activities and services. Age-friendly cities or communities benefit everybody, as they help increase economic activity, especially businesses for older persons.[35] However, most Thais do not have age-friendly housing, and knowledge about how to modify homes to be age-friendly is limited among Thai families.[36] Nevertheless, age-friendly accommodations have started to emerge in the real estate market, and the government plans to provide more of this type of housing for older persons. In addition, allowances of up to B20,000 per household are available to help communities renovate the homes of older persons in order to make the homes safe and suitable for their physical needs.[37]

---

[34]   S. Yotphet et al. 2009. *Model of Good Practice in Caring for Older Persons by Family and Rural Community in Thailand.* Bangkok: TGRI/Health Systems Research Institute of Thailand.

[35]   P. Chapon, coordinator, and E. Rosenberg, translator. 2013. *Adapting Cities to Aging: Issues of Development and Governance.* Paris: Center for Strategic Analysis; and WHO. 2007. *Global Age-Friendly Cities: A Guide.* Geneva.

[36]   T. Charuthat. 2005. *Minimum Standards of Housing and Environment for the Elderly* [in Thai]. Bangkok: Chulalongkorn University, Faculty of Architecture.

[37]   S. Chunharas, ed. 2008. *Situation of the Thai Elderly 2007.* Bangkok: TGRI.

3.2.3.5 Transport

The Thai Ministry of Transportation has studied accessibility to public transport (including buses, trains, and airports), including wheelchair lifts for public buses. Its minister announced in August 2017 his commitment to inclusive design for public transportation and facilities. The ministry has developed standards for transportation facilities, provides curricula and training for standard auditors, and offers facilitators for older persons and anyone with disabilities. This work has built on the experience of developed countries in developing practical and safe solutions.

3.3 Policy and Regulatory Structure

3.3.1   The Constitution

The Constitution of Thailand Buddhist Era (B.E.) 2560 (2017) offers the right to public health services for all Thai people. The Thai Constitution is also the supreme legal framework, and thus ensures the rights of older persons as well.

Table 8: Legal Framework Affecting Older Persons in Thailand

Year	Official Name of Law or Regulation
2017	Constitution of the Kingdom of Thailand B.E. 2560 (2017)
2015	Reorganization of Ministry, Sub-Ministry, and Department Act B.E. 2558 (2015)[a]
2010	Act on the Elderly (Issue 2) B.E. 2553 (2010 A.D.)
2003	Act on the Elderly B.E. 2546 (2003 A.D.)
2002	National Health Security Act B.E. 2545 (2002)
1999	Determining Plans and Process of Decentralization Act B.E. 2542 (1999)

A.D. = anno Domini, B.E. = Buddhist Era.

[a] This act established the Department of Older Persons.

Source: Ministry of Social Development and Human Security, Department of Elderly Affairs. Laws. http://www.dop.go.th/en/laws/2.

3.3.2   Legislation

There are many acts that are relevant to the care of older persons (Table 8). The most important of these are the Act on the Elderly B.E. 2546 (2003), the National Health Security Act B.E. 2545 (2002), and the Determining Plans and Process of Decentralization Act B.E. 2542 (1999).

The Act on the Elderly B.E. 2546 (2003) ensures that older persons have the right to health services, employment opportunities, social participation, waived fees for public services, appropriate accommodations, and a monthly pension of B600–B1,000. The Act established the National Committee on the Elderly (NCE), an inter-sector committee chaired by the Prime Minister, with a secretariat function provided by the government's lead agency. The NCE has the authority, as designated by the cabinet, to establish policies, principal plans, and a framework for providing support and assistance to older persons; and to establish the regulations involving the administration of the Elderly Fund, the approval of payments, the preparation of reports, and the receipt of monies and payments, as well as other related regulations. It is also tasked with proposing recommendations and presenting observations to the cabinet, with presenting the situation of the older persons of Thailand to the cabinet at least once a year, and with considering any other matters concerning older persons, pursuant to this act or other laws.

The National Health Security Act B.E. 2545 (2002) established universal health coverage. There are three major schemes providing health care in Thailand—the Civil Servant Medical Benefit Scheme for central government civil servants, retirees, and their dependents; the SSS for employees of private companies; and the Universal Coverage Scheme (UCS) for the remainder of the population that are not otherwise covered.

The Determining Plans and Process of Decentralization Act B.E. 2542 (1999) determined the process of decentralization, including the delegation of public service delivery, including health care and social care, to local authorities; as well as the reallocation of taxes and duties between central government and the local authorities, and among the local authorities. The role of local authorities in providing social services for older persons is explained in this act.

3.3.3   Policy Landscape: Laws and Plans for Older Persons

The Government of Thailand has adopted several policies and plans for its aging population, and it works closely with civil society on aging-related issues.[38]

The First National Long-Term Plan for Older Persons (1986–2001) was influenced by the first World Assembly on Ageing, in Vienna in 1982, and the main features of this plan were based on recommendations of the 1983 Vienna International Plan of Action on Aging. The objectives of the First National Long-Term Plan were to (i) provide older persons with general knowledge on the changes that come with age and the necessary environmental adjustments, including in health care; (ii) provide older persons with the protection and support of families and communities, including from welfare services; (iii) support the role of older persons as participants in family and other activities; and (iv) support society's responsibility for older persons. But the plan had some weaknesses. It did not include actual policies to prepare people for old age, improve their self-care, boost their social participation, strengthen family values, and integrate relationships; nor did it include strategies for sustaining family support for older persons. Specific long-term policies and measures for older persons were included, however, in the 8th National Economic and Social Development Plan (1997–2001), which featured a section on the provision of social welfare benefits to older persons.[39]

The Second National Long-Term Plan for Older Persons (2001–2021) was based on the principle that security in old age means security for society, not just for the individual, and it uses a life-course planning approach. This approach implies that older persons should live with their families and in their communities, and that public welfare services should meet the needs of older persons who cannot stay with their families or in their communities and have an acceptable quality of life; it also implies that the rights of older persons must be protected, especially from abuse, neglect, and violence. The Second National Long-Term Plan focuses on five integrated strategic practices:

---

[38]   S. Jitapunkul and S. Wivatvanit. 2009. National Policies and Programs for the Aging Population in Thailand. *Ageing International*. 33. pp. 62–74; and V. Prachuabmoh. 2015. A Lesson Learned from Community-Based Integrated Long-Term Care in Thailand. *Asia Pacific Journal of Social Work and Development*. 25 (4). pp. 213–224.

[39]   S. Jitapunkul, N. Chayovan, and J. Kespichayawattana. 2002. National Policies on Ageing and Long-Term Care Provision for Older Persons in Thailand. In D.R. Phillips and A.C.M. Chan, eds. *Ageing and Long-Term Care: National Policies in the Asia-Pacific*. Singapore: Institute of Southeast Asian Studies; Ottawa: International Development Research Centre.

(i) preparing people for a high-quality old age, (ii) capacity building for older persons, (iii) providing social protection for older persons, (iv) developing national policies for older persons, and (v) reviewing the state of knowledge about older persons. Although the plan was well designed, the evaluation of the performance of its first 5 years (2001–2006) found that the implementation of the strategies was unsatisfactory, especially when it came to preparing people for a high-quality old age and providing social protection for older persons.[40]

Progress in preparing people for a high-quality old age was slow and fragmented until 2016, when the government approved a budget for a community-based pilot LTC project.

Although there is no legal framework that specifies management standards, nor any comprehensive regulations for LTC in Thailand, **the promotion of high-quality care for older persons is indicated in the Act on the Elderly B.E. 2546 (2003), Section 10,** which states: "In order to protect the safety of service users, quality care must be provided which addresses physical, mental, spiritual and social needs."[41]

The Consumer Protection Act B.E. 2522 (1979) states that the quality of life for dependent older persons is a consumer right.

In 2009, the Second National Health Assembly passed two resolutions relating to social and health organizations, as follows:

Resolution 3.3 stated that institutions providing medical and nursing services must register with the Bureau of Sanatorium and Art of Healing, under the MOPH's Department of Health Service Support (DHSS), for standard monitoring.

Resolution 6 stated that the MOPH, the Thailand Nursing Council, the MSDHS, and the Ministry of Interior are requested to develop national standards and mechanisms for the care of dependent older persons, with participation from communities, local administration organizations (LAOs), and from older persons themselves. The standards should provide for the monitoring of both government and private sector activities.

These standards have been established not only to protect the rights of service users, but also to prevent the neglect or abuse of older persons.

3.3.4   Stakeholder Landscape: Leadership, Governance, and Coordination

As noted above, there is no overarching governing body responsible for LTC in Thailand. In terms of regulations, the MOPH is responsible for health care and health-care providers. For example, the preparation of regulations for residential LTC facilities under the Health Establishment Act B.E. 2559 (2015) is the responsibility of the DHSS. The MSDHS is responsible for regulating social care. The Ministry of Finance (MOF) is responsible for fiscal policy, including the financing of policies that address the aging of Thai society, regarding which the MOF has already prepared a range of measures. The Office of Insurance Commission (OIC) is responsible for regulating insurance, including LTC insurance, although its responsibility for private LTC insurance has not been finalized. The Ministry of Interior is responsible for overseeing local authorities. Challenges remain in implementing the necessary coordination between the related agencies, as required by the relevant legislation.

---

[40]   V. Prachuabmoh. 2008. *Design Monitor and Evaluation of the Second National Plan for Older Persons 2001– 2021* [in Thai]. Bangkok.

[41]   S. Sasat and T. Pukdeeprom. 2009. Nursing Home. *Journal of Population Studies.* 25 (1). pp. 45–62; S. Sasat et al. 2013. Long-Term Care Institutions in Thailand. *Journal of Health Research.* 27 (6). pp. 413–418; and S. Sasat et al. 2015. *The Development of Care Standard and Service Guideline for Dependent Older Persons in Long-Term Care Institutions in Thailand* [in Thai]. Bangkok.

The National Health Security Office (NHSO) is responsible for providing universal health coverage for the Thai people, including for community-based LTC. LAOs are expected to provide social and environmental modifications for older persons.

The NCE prepared the national plans for older persons. The second plan, covering 2001–2021, provides five strategies that aim to empower and protect older individuals and to change the system to benefit the older population. Civil society plays an active role in policy agenda setting, policy formulation, the development of the legal framework, and the implementation of policies on aging.

Civil society is involved in policy design and policy formulation. Older persons are encouraged to form elderly clubs. The Senior Citizens Council of Thailand (SCCT) is a not-for-profit organization that was established in 1989, under the Royal Patronage of Her Royal Highness the Queen Mother. The chair of the association also acts as deputy chair of the NCE. The SCCT is responsible for coordinating and helping to establish elderly clubs, which are managed by the older persons themselves. In 2018, there were 28,422 such clubs nationwide. In 2008, the MSDHS set up the National Elderly Assembly, to which representatives of elderly clubs from all the provinces are invited to voice their opinions and formulate resolutions on policies regarding older persons. Their recommendations are then sent to the NCE and to the Prime Minister for consideration for adoption as national policies.[42]

The MOPH recognizes people's participation as a critical factor for the effective coverage of health services. The South-East Asia Region of the World Health Organization (WHO) promulgated the Charter for Health Development of 1980, which followed the spirit of WHO's Alma-Ata Declaration of 1978, including the Declaration's goal of "Health for All in the Year 2000." The Thai government signed the charter and put it into practice by developing a training curriculum and manual, and then by recruiting a cadre of MOPH-registered health volunteers, which has since grown to 1 million members, to cover the Thai population of 69 million (as of 2019). Moreover, in 2002, the MSDHS initiated the Home Care Volunteers for the Elderly (HCVE) scheme, which is further detailed in subsection 3.4.3.

3.3.5   Development and Future Planning

Since 2010, LTC systems have been developed in Thailand because of the country's rapid demographic change, with increased legal and policy protections for older persons, as well as advocacy for older persons' rights by the National Elderly Assembly and other bodies. A further impetus for LTC development was a series of research studies that brought to light the need for care, the challenges facing family care, and other relevant issues.

The Twelfth National Economic and Social Development Plan (2017–2021) was designed to align with the 20-year Second National Plan for Older Persons (2001–2021). It includes policies and measures to mitigate the challenges of an aging society, such as improvements in the LTC system, the creation of age-friendly environments, and calls for further LTC-specific legislation.[43] The Twelfth Plan also initiated the Thailand 4.0 development agenda, which is the long-term strategic plan guiding the overall direction of government initiatives.

At present, the MSDHS and the MOPH are consulting with technical experts, the Thai Elderly Promotion and Health Care Association (TEPHA), and other stakeholders to prepare regulations on LTC registration and

---

[42]   V. Kasemsup et al. 2016. Thai Country Case Study. In V. Yiengprugsawan, J. Healy, and H. Kendig, eds. *Health System Responses to Population Aging and Noncommunicable Diseases in Asia. Comparative Country Studies.* 2 (2). pp. 76–110. New Delhi: WHO, Regional Office for South-East Asia (on behalf of the Asia Pacific Observatory on Health Systems and Policies).

[43]   Government of Thailand, Office of the National Economic and Social Development Board. 2017. *National Economic and Social Development Plan 12 (2017–2021).* Bangkok.

standards, including standards for quality management. The findings of many studies on LTC and care standards will contribute to the formulation of these regulations, which are planned for enactment in 2020.

The current government approved on 8 November 2016 policies proposed by the MOF to support an aging society. These include building accommodations adapted to the needs of older persons (e.g., senior living complexes), mortgage options for seniors (e.g., reverse mortgages), and measures to increase participation in the labor force by older persons. The cabinet approved the Government Savings Bank's launch of a reverse mortgage for seniors, the contracts for which expire within 20 years or when the homeowner dies. Borrowers aged 60–85 now have the right to live in their houses until the end of their contracts.

The community-based LTC model, described in more detail in the following section, is the first step in the national initiative aimed at improving the coverage of LTC services based on home- and community-care service provision. **Thailand is starting with a relatively modest program in terms of beneficiary eligibility and degree of benefits,** but the government aims for eventual nationwide coverage, and other elements of care provision will be added later on.

One key priority will be to integrate health and social care into the LTC system. A memorandum of understanding has already been circulated among ministers in the central government and among representatives of local governments to improve cooperation between sectors.

The government is in the process of improving the quality of LTC in Thailand. A working group is drafting national standards for LTC facilities, the nonprofessional care workforce, and their training curricula. There is a proposal under consideration to establish a National Committee on the Quality of Long-Term Care, which would work to establish national standards for quality management, including for LTC service providers, as well as a training curriculum and certification process for the care workforce. Moreover, the existing laws and regulations related to LTC are under review, and may be replaced or revised in the near future.

3.4   Service Provision

Adequate LTC requires a combination of services delivered in an integrated way and tailored to individual needs.[44] Service provision should respond to an assessment of an individual's physical, mental, and emotional situation, including the medical and psychosocial history, social and family relationships, former occupation, community involvement, and leisure and cultural activities. Also to be considered is the individual's own preferences regarding what he or she would like to be able to do without the help of the individual's support network (e.g., family, friends, neighbors, medical care, and social services). While self-care and family care may account for most care provision, a wide range of LTC services addressing needs across a continuum of care may become a necessity. At a minimum, an LTC system should be able to ensure that people have access to the care support services that they need in terms of types of services, the location of services, and affordability.

3.4.1   Types of Care Provision

The mix of care services and service providers varies from country to country. In Thailand, while it is generally the families that assist older persons with the activities of daily living (ADL), limited health and social support is provided by government institutions at the community and provincial levels. Of note, the government is investing

---

[44]   D.A. Singh. 2016. *Effective Management of Long-Term Care Facilities.* Third Edition. Burlington, MA: Jones & Bartlett Learning. Part I: Introduction to Long-Term Care, pp. 1–72.

in the development and expansion of a pilot community-care model. In addition, older persons' clubs have regular meetings and social activities, as well as coordinating assistance with health or social care and helping people get to their appointments on time.[45] Religious organizations and charities provide support to people who need LTC. Other civil society groups provide a variety of care services, often free of charge. High-quality services with a wider variety of offerings are available, mainly in the urban centers, for those who can afford it. However, as mentioned in the discussion on the supply of care (section 3.2), existing services are limited in coverage and are available only to a minority of those with severe or high dependency needs.

3.4.2 Community-Based Long-Term Care Initiatives

For 15 years, Thailand has explored models of home- and community-based care, with an emphasis on services provided at home. In 1999, a family-level social security survey found that 253,360 families, accounting for 7.5 % of the total senior population, included dependent older persons, but had no caregivers.

3.4.2.1 Home Care Volunteers for the Elderly

In 2003, the MSDHS established the HCVE project for dependent older persons in eight provinces spanning four regions. In 2007, the NCE resolved to scale up the initiative to make it nationwide, and the cabinet endorsed the pilot project as part of the National Policy on Older Persons, with the LAOs named as the main bodies responsible for implementation, but with the participation of other government agencies, civil society organizations, and community-based organizations—enabled by technical support from the MSDHS. The MSDHS extended the activities of the program by expanding the community-level networks to protect older persons' rights. As of 2020, this cadre numbers 80,000 trained volunteers, and reaches almost 800,000 people.

All volunteers receive 18 hours of training. They are responsible for at least five older persons who have no other caregivers, have been neglected, are poor, or live alone. They provide supervision and general assistance, if required, for up to 15 older persons. The volunteers receive a small monthly transport allowance.

The scope of services provided by the HCVE includes home visits, assistance with meals and eating, assistance with taking medicine, assistance with physical exercise, accompanying older persons on visits to the doctor, consultations with the doctor for instructions on providing care at home, taking older persons to community activities, taking them to recreational activities outside the house, taking them to participate in religious rites, assisting in the improvement of the house and environment, gathering older persons to participate in group activities, providing knowledge to older persons and their families, providing counseling if needed, providing information on the rights of older persons, providing information on useful services, coordinating with other organizations in support of older persons, collecting data on older persons, looking out for problems that may arise for older persons, helping older persons run errands or undertaking them on their behalf, and organizing useful activities for older persons.[46] In addition, the HCVE has to record the personal information of the older persons under its care, such as their level of dependency, their problems and needs, and the services being provided to them.

---

[45]   S. Yodpet et al. 2012. *Operation and Activities of Elderly Clubs* [in Thai]. Bangkok: TGRI and the Thai Health Foundation.

[46]   S. Sasat and V. Chuangwiwat. 2013. *Approaches to Home and Community Care Programme for Older People: Thailand Experience*. Paper prepared for the Asia-Pacific Expert Meeting on Long-term Care and China/ESCAP "Strengthening National Capacity for Promoting and Protecting the Rights of Older Persons" Project Launching Meeting. Shanghai. 18–19 December; and W. Suwanrada et al. 2016. *Evaluation of the Replication Project of the Elderly Home Care Volunteers* [in Thai]. Bangkok: Chulalongkorn University, College of Population Studies.

However, the care provided by the HCVE volunteers has been inconsistent, with only 33% of participating districts in 2013 reporting that the care provided was sufficient to meet their older persons' LTC needs, and then only for those with mild or moderate ADL limitations.[47] In fact, based on the 2017 Survey of the Older Persons in Thailand of the National Statistical Office (NSO), only 17.9% of older persons had had a visit from a volunteer during the previous year.

The responsibility for managing HCVE volunteers has been gradually transferred to the LAOs. Despite the expectation that the volunteers would provide basic health care and personal care for dependent older persons, their help is usually limited to home visits, psychosocial support, and referring cases to responsible bodies.

A supplementary project initiated by the SCCT was Friends Help Friends, financially supported by the Thai Health Promotion Foundation. The project aimed to maximize the support of active old-age groups for dependent older persons in the community. The volunteers, most of whom were members of older persons' clubs, were trained to provide basic health care, rehabilitation, and social support to dependent older persons who lacked family caregivers; in practice, however, the Friends Help Friends volunteers mainly provided psychosocial support. By 2008, there were 8,074 volunteers; the majority of them came from 376 older persons' clubs, but there were also 2,936 volunteers from other age groups, and together they served 7,360 older persons who needed home visits (footnote 40). In 2009, the responsibility for Friends Help Friends was transferred to the LAOs, and since then the project's ongoing effectiveness has depended on the LAOs' interest and capacity. Due to the LAOs' lack of interest and funding, however, the project has been gradually winding down, thereby highlighting the need for dependable sources of funding for such initiatives.

3.4.2.2   Integrated Community-Based Care Pilot Projects

In 2007, the MSDHS monitored and evaluated the implementation of the Second National Plan for Older Persons, and a first revision was issued in 2009. The revised plan recommended the development of health and social services for older persons, including a community-based LTC system.

The Japan International Cooperation Agency (JICA) supported the development of community-based LTC in Thailand. A project thus began in 2007 as a collaboration between JICA, the MOPH, and the MSDHS. The first phase of the project (2007–2011), "Development of a Community-Based, Integrated Health Care and Social Welfare Services Model for Thai Older Persons," assessed the situation of aging, policies, welfare, and social support systems in Thailand, and piloted LTC models in selected sites. The second phase (2013–2017), "Long-Term Care Service Development for the Frail Elderly and Other Vulnerable People" (LTOP), developed evidence-based policy recommendations for LTC that targeted frail older persons.[48]

In 2013, the Department of Health and the MOPH launched a pilot project in selected provinces that established a care-management system for community-based LTC. The project, Community Health Promotion Hospitals, has taken the lead in managing at-home care. This initiative has applied findings from the LTOP project, and made great strides toward the further development of Thailand's LTC system.

---

[47]   S. Lakbenjakul. 2013. *Integrated Long-Term Care System, "Lamsonthi Model": Principle, Process and Performance.* Nonthaburi, Thailand: Health Insurance System Research Office and Health Systems Research Institute of Thailand; P. Lloyd-Sherlock et al. 2017. Volunteer Provision of Long-Term Care for Older People in Thailand and Costa Rica. *Bulletin of the World Health Organization.* 95 (11). pp. 774–778; and S. Yodpet et al. 2012. *Operation and Activities of Elderly Clubs* [in Thai]. Bangkok: TGRI and the Thai Health Foundation.

[48]   Y. Okumoto. 2015. *Responding to Ageing Society in Asia: JICA's Work and Experience.* Tokyo: JICA, Office for Gender Equality and Poverty Reduction. https://jaww.info/okumotoRespondingtoageingsocietyinAsia150310new.pdf; and JICA. 2018. *The Challenge of an Aging Society in Asia: The JICA Approach to Long-term Care; Welfare Services for the Elderly.* Tokyo.

Building on previous efforts to improve LTC services, the government launched in 2016 pilot project "Development of a Public Health LTC System for Dependent Older People in LTC Subdistricts." This project aims to establish a care-management system for community-based LTC, and it is managed by the National Health Security Office (NHSO) and local authorities (Figure 5). A care manager, usually a nurse from the Community Health Promotion Hospitals, assesses the care needs of a dependent older person, and this assessment serves as the basis for an individual care plan that is drawn up at a multidisciplinary team meeting. The care manager then assigns and supervises a volunteer caregiver who provides services according to the individual's care plan. In its first year, the central government provided B600 million through the NHSO to support this project. Of this amount, B500 million went to the Local Health Fund to support care provision at home, and B100 million went to the country's primary care units for human capacity building, including care-management and volunteer-caregiver training.[49] The pilot project intends to reach 100,000 older persons with a high degree of frailty (13 or higher on the Barthel Index) and to provide assessments, case management, and home visits by caregivers lasting 2–8 hours a week, depending on the need and availability of care support. In 2017, the program budget was increased to B900 million, to enable the project to reach 150,000 people, and in 2018, it was raised to B1.159 billion, to enable the project to reach 193,200 people. As of 2018, there were 72,000 trained caregivers participating in this project.

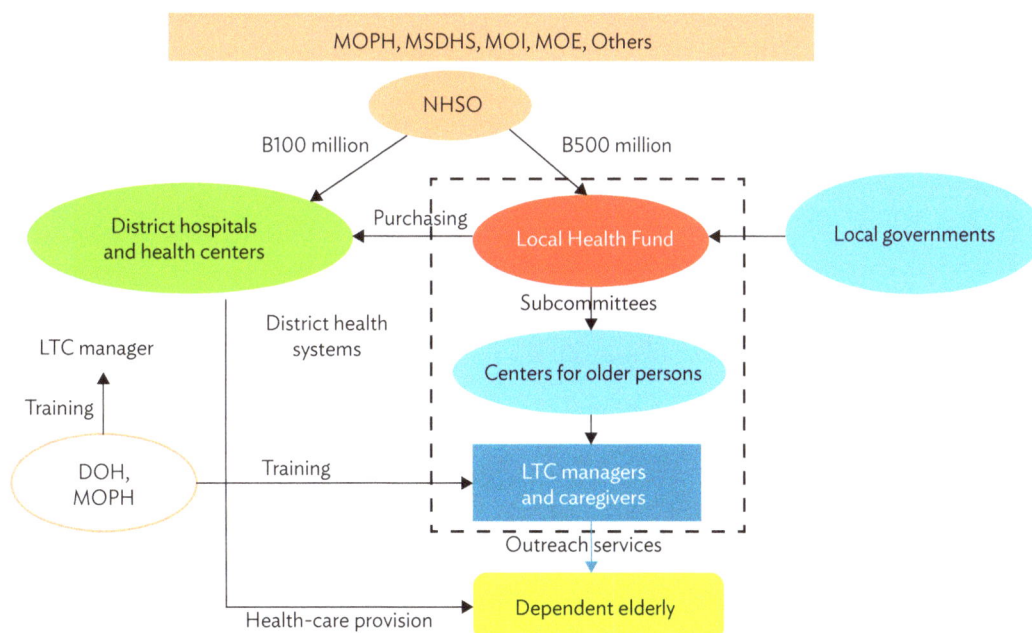

Figure 5: Coordination of Agencies Working on Long-Term Care

B = baht (Thai currency), DOH = Department of Health, LTC = long-term care, MOE = Ministry of Education, MOI = Ministry of Interior, MOPH = Ministry of Public Health, MSDHS = Ministry of Social Development and Human Security, NHSO = National Health Security Office.

Source: A. Amorim and Hoang Viet Tran, eds. 2018. *South-South and Triangular Cooperation and the Care Economy*. Geneva: International Labour Organization. p. 44.

---

[49]   Government of Thailand, NHSO. 2016b. *Proclamation of the National Health Security Office on Criteria for Supporting the Administration of a Local Authority on the Local Health Security Fund (Revision 2)*. Bangkok.

3.4.3   Long-Term Care Benefits Packages for Dependent Older Persons

Benefits packages for dependent older persons include medical services (e.g., screening examinations), care needs assessment, home visits, health-promotion and preventive services, physiotherapy, occupational therapy, and the provision of rehabilitative and assistive devices as defined either by the Sub-Committee for the Development of a Long-Term Care System for Dependent Older People or by the NSHO.

Also included in the benefits packages are social services such as assistance with housework or ADL, the provision of social assistance equipment, and assistance in performing activities outside the home.[50]

Table 9: Groups Eligible for Benefits Packages

Group 1	Group 2	Group 3	Group 4
Being able to partially move, having some eating or elimination disorder, no cognitive disorder	Having a cognitive disorder	Not able to move, having some eating or elimination disorder, or severe diseases	Have a serious illness for which only palliative care can be given
Budget: < B4,000	Budget: B3,000–B6,000	Budget: B4,000–B8,000	Budget: B5,000–B10,000

B = baht (Thai currency).
Note: The budgets are per person per year.
Source: Government of Thailand, National Health Security Office.

The NHSO has developed a manual to assess dependency levels for community-based LTC (footnote 44). This manual was modified based on various international-standard tools such as the Mini-Mental State Examination and the Barthel Index (which measures performance on ADL).

An impact evaluation of the pilot project for the Community-Based Long-Term Care Program has yet to be carried out, but an initial evaluation was conducted after 2 years of implementation. Selected findings from that evaluation are as follows:

(i)   The Local Health Fund is an appropriate mechanism for managing community-based LTC, as it can generate cooperation across sectors.

(ii)   In practice, there were challenges in integrating home health-care and LTC services, and only in two areas (in Lumsonthi and Kuchinarai districts, where they had previously conducted pilots) was there successfully integrated and coordinated people-centered care.

(iii)   Health-care services are provided in a more regular and systematic way than are social care services. The service provided least often was social care for the instrumental activities of daily living (IADL), economic support, legal support, and fall prevention (only in 10%–30% of cases).

(iv)   The MOPH preferred that care be provided by volunteer caregivers, while the NHSO recommended paid caregivers. Most local areas used volunteer caregivers. However, the evaluation found that paid caregivers performed at a higher standard in all main areas of care service provision. Furthermore, there were difficulties with recruitment, the quality of care, and the management of unpaid caregivers.

---

[50]   NHSO. 2016a. *Manual for the Administration of Health Care in Long-Term Care Services for Older People Living with Dependency under the Universal Health Coverage Scheme* [in Thai]. Bangkok.

(v)   The unclear division of financial responsibilities between the NHSO and the local governments delayed and limited the implementation of the project.

(vi)   Only those individuals over 60 who are covered by the Universal Coverage Scheme (UCS) are eligible for LTC under the project. Those with the UCS coverage who are under 60 and those covered under the Social Security Scheme (SSS) or by private insurance cannot receive these LTC services. It is anticipated that, when implemented nationally, the project will only cover 60%–70% of those who have high ADL or IADL support needs.[51]

In summary, the development of various community-based LTC initiatives provides some useful lessons for other countries. The home care services from the MSDHS focused on social care, while the services from the MOPH focused on health care. Recent projects and programs have specialized in integrating service delivery, and their efforts have highlighted the challenges of effective collaboration between departments with different budget lines and mandates, as well as the challenges in striking the appropriate balance between health care and social care.

3.4.4 Day Care

Adult day care—a service that can supplement family care; provide trained care for large numbers of older persons; and promote social participation, as well as cognitive, physical, and emotional wellness—is currently under experimentation. The MSDHS offers a limited number of day care services to adults with moderate care needs who already receive family care at home.[52] In addition, some local municipalities and health authorities have established day care centers for dependent older persons, to boost their functional recovery or to provide a respite to family caregivers. Private businesses, mainly in Bangkok, also provide day care services for a fee. Day care is a promising area because its support extends to the older persons' families, and because it promotes active aging and preventive activities for older persons with a low or moderate degree of care needs.

3.4.5 Residential Long-Term Care

National strategies for the health-care and social-care systems, including community-based LTC systems, aim to promote aging in place. Most residential care services for dependent older persons are found in private nursing homes and private hospitals, although some residential homes and homes for poor older persons are financed by the government and charitable organizations. Services at these facilities range from basic to complex care, including accommodations, help with personal hygiene, assistance with ADL and moving about, care that requires nursing skills, rehabilitation, day care, respite care, and hospice care (footnote 25).

An initial study by Sasat et al., conducted in 2009, classified residential LTC in Thailand into five categories, according to the objectives of each service: residential home, assisted living, nursing home, LTC hospital, and hospice care (footnote 28). However, to respond more effectively to the problems and care needs of older persons, another 2009 study, by Sasat, Choowattanapakorn, and Lertrat, classified residential LTC into two categories: low care and high care.[53]

---

[51]   S. Srithamrongsawat. 2017. *National Consultation on the Country Diagnostic Study Draft for Thailand.* Presentation of an evaluation of community-based long-term care implementation in Thailand. Bangkok. 15 September 2017.

[52]   TGRI. 2009. *Situation of the Thai Elderly 2008.* Bangkok. See similar findings in JICA. 2018. *The Challenge of an Aging Society in Asia: The JICA Approach to Long-term Care : Welfare Services for the Elderly.* Tokyo.

[53]   S. Sasat, T. Choowattanapakorn, and P. Lertrat. 2009. *A Model of Institutional Long-Term Care for Older Persons in Thailand.* Nonthaburi, Thailand: Health Systems Research Institute of Thailand.

3.4.5.1 Low (or Basic) Care

Low care, also called "basic care," is a service that focuses on social care and welfare for older persons, with an emphasis on providing shelter. It includes assistance with ADL or assisted living, but not medical care. Instead, the focus is on assistance with eating, moving about, and using assistive devices to get around. At assisted-living facilities, most residents do not need a medical doctor. Responsibility rests mainly with a social worker, but also with an occupational therapist, a nutritionist, maybe one or two registered nurses, care workers of lower status than that of a nurse, and maybe a physiotherapist. Although there is no doctor involved in basic care, older persons regularly receive medication based on previous prescriptions for chronic diseases. In the case of illness, older persons are assisted with the traveling they must do to receive a diagnosis, treatment, or medication, or to see a doctor as required.

3.4.5.2 High Care

High care is the level of care for older persons who have a chronic illness; are dependent; and who require skilled nursing, close supervision, follow-up, and further medical treatment. LTC institutions that provide a high level of care include nursing homes, hospitals, and hospices. Services include rehabilitation, maintaining body functions, and palliative care (e.g., medication to relieve pain). Hospice care provides palliative care for people with incurable chronic diseases requiring no intervention besides helping patients to relax and be free from pain and suffering, or holistic care that emphasizes spiritual care. Palliative care requires skilled and experienced care personnel.

Although there are no public nursing homes in Thailand, public residential homes for vulnerable, active older persons also provide care for frail and bedridden residents who have no specialized staff or facilities to assist them.[54] In the entire country, there are only 12 public residential homes provided by the MSDHS and 13 residential homes provided by local authorities (footnote 20).

In 2008, a large-scale survey was conducted of residential LTCs for older persons (60 years and above) in Thailand (footnote 36). The findings revealed that there were 138 residential LTC facilities, of which 43.48% were nursing homes, 31.88% were residential homes, 18.12% were LTC hospitals, 4.35% were assisted-living centers, and 2.17% were hospices. Of these facilities, 49.28% were located in Bangkok and 45.50% were not registered.

A later study on the demand for LTC services for **older persons in Bangkok found that older persons who stayed in nursing homes did so mainly because their families were unable to take care of them and because skilled care personnel was needed**.[55] Most of those needing a high level of care were bedridden and unable to communicate. Since there is no public nursing home available in Thailand, family income is the main financial resource and a crucial factor in acquiring access to private nursing home care.

In 2016, the Department of Business Development of the Ministry of Commerce (MOC) reported that there were 442 private facilities that had registered to open a business to provide care for older persons (footnote 3). Two-thirds were private businesses and one-third (144 facilities) were corporations. There were 10 facilities under non-Thai ownership, and these were not classified by type of service. The number of private facilities reported was probably lower than the actual number, as there is no legal requirement for LTC facilities to register their types of

---

[54]   S. Sasat et al. 2015. *The Development of Care Standard and Service Guideline for Dependent Older Persons in Long-Term Care Institution* [in Thai]. Presentation at the Nursing Home Research International Working Groups. Toulouse, France. 2–3 December.

[55]   W. Suwanrada, S. Sasat, and S. Kumruangrit. 2010. Demand for Long-Term Care Service for Older Persons in Bangkok. *Journal of Economic and Public Policy*. 1 (1). pp. 20–41.

services. These facilities can register with the MOC under other categories. It is encouraging that business owners gathered to form the Thai Elderly Promotion and Health Care Association (TEPHA), which had 110 members as of 2016. The MOC's Business Development Department also promotes the growth of the medical and health-care businesses for foreign clients, recognizing the potential market for medical tourism and retirement services.[56]

3.4.6   Assistive Devices

In Thailand, there is insufficient provision of assistive devices, although access to common devices, such as eyeglasses, has been increasing. Initiatives such as the partnership between the Thai Red Cross and the Top Charoen Optic Company to provide free eye testing, eyeglasses, and cataract surgery to people in rural areas, which ran from 2009 to 2019, have contributed to the increase in access.

In accordance with the Persons with Disabilities Empowerment Act B.E. 2550 (2007), a social health protection scheme provides assistive devices to persons with disabilities, based on a doctor's assessment.[57] There are also charities and other organizations providing assistive devices. For example, a Bangkok-based nongovernment organization (NGO), forOldy, has opened a shop called "Grandma's," which sells or provides secondhand assistive equipment to older persons. It is a social enterprise that helps the poor to obtain necessary assistive devices such as walkers, canes, wheelchairs, and patient beds.

3.5 Quality Management

"Quality" refers to the extent to which a service increases the probability of desired outcomes and reduces the probability of undesired outcomes, given the limitations of existing knowledge.[58] The most common framework for evaluating the quality of care is that of Donabedian (1980, 1986, and 1988) who conceptualized three dimensions: structure (the attributes of the location where the care is delivered), process (whether or not good medical practices are followed), and outcome (impact of the care on health status).[59]

3.5.1   Registration of Care Providers

Currently, one of the key challenges in ensuring quality care is offered and maintained by service providers is that many LTC providers are either registered under different government bodies, depending on whether they are public or private institutions, and what services they provided. Many are not registered at all. For example, private agencies that provide care for older persons are meant to be registered with the MOC as businesses. However, a recent 2020 study on residential LTC institutions in Bangkok found that many residential facilities were neither registered nor following quality-care regulations. This obviously raises concerns about the quality of care, especially given the increasing number of small private care providers.[60] Starting in January 2020, under the

---

[56]   P. Pratruangkrai. 2016. Thailand Can Be Centre for Elderly Care. *The Nation Thailand.* 18 July. https://www.nationthailand.com/business/30290874.

[57]   The Persons with Disabilities Empowerment Act B.E. 2550 (2007). http://dep.go.th/sites/default/files/files/news/2.pdf.

[58]   G. Harman. 1996. *Quality Assurance for Higher Education: Developing and Managing Quality Assurance for Higher Education Systems and Institutions in Asia and the Pacific.* Bangkok: United Nations Educational, Scientific and Cultural Organization (UNESCO) Principal Regional Office for Asia and the Pacific.

[59]   A. Donabedian. 1985. Twenty Years of Research on the Quality of Medical Care: 1964–1984. *Evaluation & the Health Professions.* 8 (3). pp. 243–265.

[60]   P. Lloyd-Sherlock et al. 2020. The Rapid Expansion of Residential Long-Term Care Services in Bangkok: A Challenge For Regulation. *University of East Anglia Working Paper Series.* 55. January. Norwich, United Kingdom: University of East Anglia, School of International Development.

Health Establishment Act, the MOPH is responsible for the registration of all home and residential care service providers to consolidate the registration system.

3.5.2 Quality Standards

The Department of Health Service Support (DHSS), under the MOPH, is responsible for drafting the national standards, and for certifying LTC services in Thailand. Based on academic studies (Sasat 2012), stakeholder consultations, and public hearings, standards for LTC services have been drafted under three categories: structure including the domains of physical environment, staff, and management; process including the domains of care service, safety of care, and participation; and outcomes focused on the levels of satisfaction with care.

3.6 Human Resources

3.6.1   Who Provides Care?

There are several types of people providing care to the elderly, depending on the social context, the problems involved, the need for care, the conditions under which the care is given, and policy influences. Having sufficient numbers of trained caregivers at various levels of qualification is key to ensuring good-quality and accessible LTC services for older persons.

The care workforce can be categorized into two major groups—formal carers or caregivers and informal carers—and the structure of these groups can be visualized according to the classifications in Figure 6.

3.6.1.1   Informal Carers and Caregivers

Informal systems of social and economic exchange within families are critical to maintaining the well-being of older persons in Thailand. Usually, children are the main source of income for older persons, and very few older parents appear to be abandoned by their children because, according to a 2011 survey, 98% of older persons either lived with or next to a child, or at least had monthly visits or phone calls from a child.[61]

In general, care for older persons in Thailand is provided by informal caregivers. In the Thai context, the term "informal caregiver" refers to people who have never been trained, but who assist older persons with their activities of daily living (ADL). These caregivers can be classified by the amount of care they provide. Those who devote the highest amount of time to caring are classified as "primary caregivers," while others are classified as "secondary caregivers" or "helpers." Evidence from the 2011 survey shows that among the older persons who received daily care from caregivers, family members were the primary caregivers, including daughters (52%), grandchildren (37%), sons (36%), sons-in-law or daughters-in-law (35%), spouses (25%), and siblings (19%) (footnote 61).

Family members also tend to be the main secondary caregivers, while informal helpers can include other relatives, friends, or neighbors who provide voluntary assistance with household chores or ADL. In fact, older persons may

---

[61]   J. Knodel, V. Prachmuabmoh, and N. Chayovan. 2013. *The Changing Well-Being of Thai Elderly: An Update from the 2011 Survey of Older Persons in Thailand*. Chiang Mai, Thailand: HelpAge International; and J. Knodel et al. 2015. The Situation of Thailand's Older Population: An Update Based on the 2014 Survey of Older Persons in Thailand. *Research Collection School of Social Sciences*. Paper 1948. Singapore: Singapore Management University.

Figure 6: Care Workforce Categorization

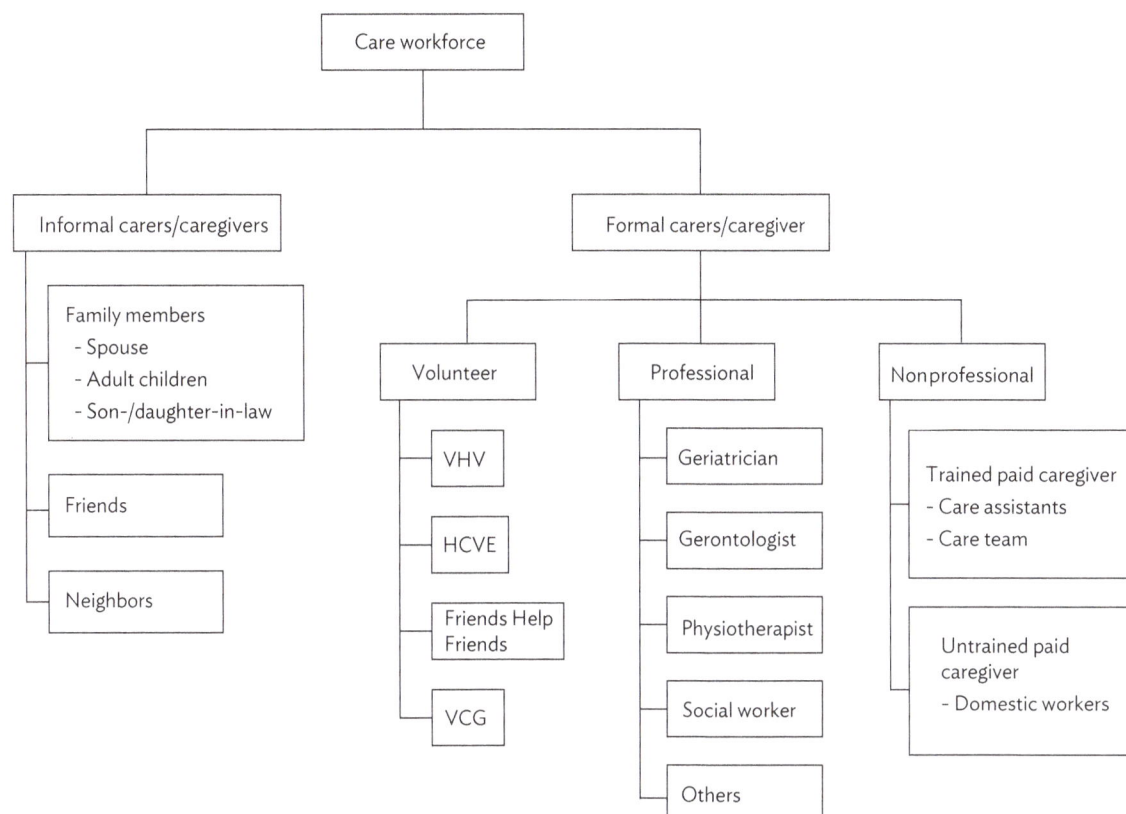

```
                                    Care workforce
                    ┌───────────────────┴───────────────────┐
          Informal carers/caregivers              Formal carers/caregiver
                    │                    ┌──────────────┼──────────────┐
          ┌─ Family members          Volunteer     Professional    Nonprofessional
          │   - Spouse                  │              │                │
          │   - Adult children       ┌─ VHV        ┌─ Geriatrician   ┌─ Trained paid caregiver
          │   - Son-/daughter-in-law │             │                 │   - Care assistants
          │                          ├─ HCVE       ├─ Gerontologist  │   - Care team
          ├─ Friends                 │             │                 │
          │                          ├─ Friends Help├─ Physiotherapist├─ Untrained paid
          └─ Neighbors               │   Friends   │                 │   caregiver
                                     └─ VCG        ├─ Social worker   │   - Domestic workers
                                                   │
                                                   └─ Others
```

HCVE = Home Care Volunteers for the Elderly, VCG = volunteer caregiver, VHV = village health volunteer.

Source: S. Sasat. 2012. *Quality of Care Development for Dependent Older Persons in Long-Term Care Institutions: Knowledge, Attitude and Practice of Nursing Staff.* Bangkok.

be getting 24 hours of care support per day from informal caregivers without pay. This kind of dedicated care owes much to love, friendship, a sense of responsibility, and/or gratitude.

However, this kind of care is also associated with stress and other difficulties for the caregivers. In 2009, a survey of older persons in the Bangkok Metropolitan Area found that caring caused a worsening of physical health in 10% of informal caregivers due to inadequate rest. [62] Also, distress and mental health deterioration occurred in around 10% of informal caregivers, as a result of older persons' difficult behavior and the fact that the caregivers had insufficient money for daily living.[63] A 2010 survey focusing on older persons from middle-income families in 10 provinces found that 1% of informal caregivers of older persons had to quit their jobs, and 29%

---

[62] W. Suwanrada, S. Sasat, and S. Kamruangrit. 2009. *Financing Long Term Care Services for the Elderly in the Bangkok Metropolitan Administration.* Research report submitted to the TGRI and to the Thai Health Promotion Foundation. Bangkok.

[63] This study in the Bangkok Metropolitan Area used a multistage sampling frame based on government registers of the Bangkok Metropolitan Area. The collected sample comprised 1,297 households, which included 1,623 older persons (60 years old and above). Among the older persons in the sample, 90.1% were independent and 4.1% were totally dependent.

were themselves over 60.[64] The survey's findings were similar to those of the 2009 survey in that the informal caregivers had both physical and mental problems as a result of caring for older persons with disabilities.

Most community-based care in Thailand focuses on family caregivers and volunteers. And most capacity building has been provided to volunteers quite systematically, with progressive improvements, while little has been done for the family caregivers, despite the fact that they are generally the primary caregivers.[65]

3.6.1.2 Formal Carers and Caregivers

Formal carers or caregivers are those who have been trained and/or receive payment for the services they provide. There has been an increasing trend toward hiring formal caregivers to look after older persons at home, as the supply of informal carers has been decreasing due to such factors as migration for work and female workforce participation.

Formal caregivers or care workers typically come from outside the network of family, friends, and neighbors. They also encompass a wide variety of personnel, including medical doctors, nurses, physiotherapists, occupational therapists, and other health professionals, in addition to care assistants from care service providers and volunteers who provide care at home. The range of formal caregivers is described below in more detail, in terms of classification, characteristics, responsibilities, and training.

Volunteers. After family caregivers, volunteers are the next most important group. Volunteers have been officially trained in the basics of caring for older persons. Although they work without pay, those who volunteer for government projects receive transport allowances. The roughly 1 million village health volunteers (VHVs) in Thailand play an important role in the country's care ecosystem, but they do not have any specific responsibility or training for LTC.

The two main government programs that utilize volunteer caregivers are described in section 3.4 (on service provision). One is the Home Care Volunteers for the Elderly (HCVE); the other is the Community-Based Long-Term Care Program, under the National Health Security Office (NHSO), which uses volunteer caregivers in about 75% of the participating districts and paid caregivers in the other 25%. The HCVE volunteers are trained for 3 days, for a total of 18 hours, in basic personal care of older persons, the role of the volunteer, welfare and social services for older persons, and health promotion for older persons. The caregivers involved in the Community-Based Long-Term Care Program receive 70 hours of training based on MOPH guidelines, whether they are volunteers or paid caregivers.[66] More details on the curricula of both programs can be found in section 3.6.6 (on training and qualifications).

---

[64] The 2010 survey, published by W. Suwanrada et al. in *Long-Term Care System for Old-Age Security Promotion*, used a multistage sampling frame based on government registers. The total sample comprised 1,297 households, which included 1,363 older middle income people (60 years old and above) in 10 provinces. See W. Suwanrada et al. 2010. *Long-Term Care System for Old-Age Security Promotion* [in Thai]. Bangkok: Ministry of Social Development and Human Security, Office of the Welfare Promotion Protection and Empowerment of Vulnerable Groups. It should be noted that the designation of older persons as "middle income" applies to those with an income higher than the national poverty line (B1,443 per month in 2010). This definition of middle income, developed by the researchers, was based on a consideration of the median income and the large proportion of households with incomes from the agriculture or informal sector. It should be noted that the minimum wage, B150–B206 per day in 2010, was higher than the median income of Thai households.

[65] S. Sasat and V. Chuangwiwat. 2013. *Approaches to Home and Community Care Programme for Older People: Thailand Experience.* Paper prepared for the Asia-Pacific Expert Meeting on Long-term Care and China/ESCAP "Strengthening National Capacity for Promoting and Protecting the Rights of Older Persons" Project Launching Meeting. Shanghai. 18–19 December.

[66] TGRI. 2017. *Situation of the Thai Elderly 2016.* Bangkok.

The extent and quality of services provided by volunteers varies across communities, however. An evaluation of HCVE services conducted by the Ministry of Social Development and Human Security (MSDHS) showed that only one-third of local authorities reported that the services provided by the HCVE—such as home visits and assistance with preparing meals and eating, taking medicine, and exercise—had met the needs of older persons in their communities (footnotes 44 and 45). The VHVs, who operate under the MOPH, provide basic health care for older persons, and they have had the same problems as the HCVE volunteers: it is difficult for them to provide regular or routine care, especially for severely dependent older persons, because they also have other roles and activities in the community (footnote 42). As mentioned previously, most districts were using volunteer caregivers, with a minority using paid caregivers. The evaluation showed that the paid caregivers outperformed the volunteer caregivers in the first 3 years of this program in all the main areas of care provision.

Professional care personnel. This is a multidisciplinary category that encompasses professionals who work in the health and social professions, including doctors, nurses, pharmacists, dentists, physiotherapists, occupational therapists, and other health personnel who receive payment for the provision of care services. Professional organizations serving these categories of health workers provide supervision and support for their members.

Geriatricians. A geriatrician is a medical doctor specializing in geriatric medicine. There were 36,938 trained medical doctors overall in Thailand in 2018.[67] The country has two institutions offering 2-year residencies in geriatrics: the Siriraj Faculty of Medicine and the Ramathibodi Faculty of Medicine, both at Mahidol University. There is no official data reporting on graduates in geriatrics, though personal interviews reveal that the Siriraj Faculty of Medicine produces 3–5 geriatricians per year and the Ramathibodi Faculty of Medicine produces 1–5 geriatricians per year.

Geriatric nurses. There were 165,541 registered nurses (with 4 years of training), 7,257 technical nurses (2 years of training) and 7,000 practical nurses (1 year of training) in Thailand in 2018 (footnote 20), but the numbers of nurses specializing in geriatrics are unavailable. There are two levels of geriatric training for nurses: a 4-month postgraduate certificate program in geriatric nursing and a 2-year master's degree in geriatric nursing. There is no PhD program in geriatric nursing, but there are a number of PhD graduates in more general fields who have focused on the aging population. There are at least five universities offering master's degrees in geriatric nursing, and each university produces 10–15 graduates per year.

The future of the master's degree in geriatric nursing is uncertain, however, because the Thailand Nursing Council supports the merging of the geriatric nursing masters with the adult nursing masters. And geriatric nursing programs are at risk because of a lack of specialized instructors. But there are plans for a master's degree in gerontology to include 4 months of postgraduate training in geriatric nursing. Most training in geriatric nursing focuses on acute care and community care, without developing the skills necessary for work in LTC facilities. Advanced nursing and research skills in this area are essential for improving the quality of care for older persons in LTC facilities.

Physiotherapists and occupational therapists. Many universities in Thailand, both private and public, offer a 4-year degree program in physiotherapy, but there were only 4,836 physiotherapists in 2018 (footnote 20). In addition, only a few universities offer a degree program in occupational therapy. As Thai society continues to age, however, the demand for occupational therapists will escalate, as they will be needed to help older persons improve their ability to engage in ADL.

---

[67]   MOPH. 2018. *Report on Public Health Resources 2018* [in Thai]. Nonthaburi, Thailand.

Social workers. The Faculty of Social Administration at Thammasat University offers a 4-year bachelor's degree with a minor in "social security for older people." This program aims to improve service delivery and assist in the development of new social welfare systems in Thailand. Recently, the Chulabhorn International College of Medicine at Thammasat University started offering a master of science in social gerontology, with the aim of encouraging and empowering young academics to do research in holistic care for older persons and come up with innovative policy ideas.

Other professionals. Many professions can contribute their expertise when it comes to caring for older persons. This includes pharmacists paying attention to polypharmacy and drug interactions in older persons; dentists with an interest in the oral health of older persons; and architects interested in age-friendly design, age-friendly environments, and age-friendly housing. There is an increasing awareness of the aging of Thai society, so most professionals have acquired knowledge relating to older persons from their academic curricula and professional training.

Nonprofessional care personnel. This group encompasses people who actually provide private care for older persons, especially at home and in the community. They do not necessarily have formal training, but use past experience in caring for their own family members or their own knowledge and skills to provide care for others. This group can be called "paid caregivers," and are classified into the following groups:

(i)   **Trained paid caregivers.** They are nonprofessional caregivers who have been trained in caring for older persons and who receive payment for their services. In general, the role of this group of caregivers is to provide personal care, such as assisting older persons in bathing, moving about, walking, exercise, and taking medicine; they can also provide home care services. Aside from those trained through the NHSO's Community-Based Long-Term Care Program, many of them are privately engaged or work through for-profit companies.

(ii)   **Care assistants.** They provide health-care assistance to older persons or to persons with disabilities. In the past in Thailand, the word "caregiver" referred to people who had undergone 420 hours (or 3 months) of training in caring for children or older persons. However, today, this term is often confused with informal caregivers, who are not professional and do not generally receive any training. Internationally, trained care workers are called "care assistants" or "health-care assistants" (footnote 56). The Department of Skills Development, at Thailand's Ministry of Labour, has changed its usage from "caregiver" to "care assistant" to avoid confusion and to comply with international terminology.

(iii) **Untrained paid caregivers.** Those people who provide assistance with ADL and household chores using their own basic skills and experience are untrained paid caregivers. In Thailand, there are paid care assistants (without certificates from caregiver training institutes) who arrange individually to work at the homes of older persons. The actual number of untrained paid caregivers is unknown, and there is no study that has focused on this group.

(iv)   **Domestic workers.** As their employers age, these workers often become their employers' caregivers, or they are hired by a family specifically to care for an older family member. However, the actual number of domestic workers providing LTC support is unknown.

The estimated and projected numbers of dependent older persons differ between government departments. Each department has introduced various projects to help the same demographic of dependent older persons. Similarly, there are no clear boundaries between the activities of different volunteer groups, which are often made up of the same people. And there are no statistics available on the actual number of formal caregivers, both professional and nonprofessional (Table 7, on page 17). Therefore, research on the role of each volunteer group, and on the numbers of formal and informal caregivers, is needed to be able to plan for future human resources development.

3.6.2   Incomes of Care Workers

Informal caregivers receive no government allowances in Thailand. Yet, caregiving duties have been an intrinsic part of family responsibilities for generations. There is no information available about the financial situation and incomes of family caregivers. This is a gap in our knowledge that requires further study to fill.

However, for formal caregivers, a survey of the salaries of care personnel published in 2009 by Sasat et al. found that most care assistants (52.8%) received monthly salaries of less than B7,000 ($200).[68] Table 10 provides a salary breakdown for care service providers working in each type of facility. For instance, most of the caregivers working in nursing homes (59.1%), in assisted-living facilities (58.3%), and in residential homes (54.4%) earned less than B7,000 per month. Table 11 provides a breakdown of salaries by occupation. It shows, for example, that the largest contingent of care personnel receiving monthly salaries of B25,001–B30,000 ($714–$857) were nurses, who accounted for 16.7 % of care providers in that salary range; they were followed by physiotherapists (12.6%) and occupational therapists (6.5%).

Table 10: Breakdown of Salaries for Care Service Providers, by Type of Residential Care Facility, 2009
(%)

Monthly Salary	Type of Residential Care Facility					Total
	Residential Home	Assisted Living	Hospital LTC Unit	Nursing Home	Hospice Care	
Less than B7,000	54.4	58.3	46.9	59.1	44.4	52.8
B7,000–B10,000	10.3	8.3	6.3	31.8	0.0	13.2
B10,001–B15,000	27.9	8.3	23.4	0.0	11.1	18.3
B15,001–B20,000	1.5	0.0	6.3	2.3	11.1	3.6
B20,001–B25,000	2.9	0.0	12.5	6.8	33.3	8.1
B25,001–B30,000	2.9	25.0	4.7	0.0	0.0	4.1
Total	100.0 (68)	100.0 (12)	100.0 (64)	100.0 (44)	100.0 (9)	100.0 (197)

B = baht (Thai currency), LTC = long-term care.
Notes:
1. Percentages may not total exactly 100% because of rounding.
2. The numbers in parentheses indicate the actual number of respondents who worked in each type of residential care facility. There were 197 respondents in all.

Source: S. Sasat et al. 2009. *Research Report on Long-Term Care Institutions in Thailand.* Nonthaburi, Thailand: Health Systems Research Institute of Thailand.

The 2009 survey by Sasat et al. also found that most of those employed by private service providers or charitable organizations received monthly salaries of less than B7,000 (66.7%); and the same was true for most of those employed by religious private service providers (62.5%) and by government service providers (56.1%) operating under a local administration organization (LAO). Among those who received monthly salaries in the B25,001–B30,000 range, the largest group worked in the government sector under the MOPH, followed by government service providers under an LAO, private service providers, and the business sector.

[68]   S. Sasat et al. 2009. *Research Report on Long-Term Care Institutions in Thailand.* Nonthaburi, Thailand: Health Systems Research Institute of Thailand; and S. Sasat et al. 2013. Long-Term Care Institutions in Thailand. *Journal of Health Research.* 27 (6). pp. 413–418.

Table 11: Breakdown of Salaries for Care Service Providers, by Occupation, 2009
(%)

Occupation	Monthly Salary Ranges						Total
	Less than B7,000	B7,000– B10,000	B10,001– B15,000	B15,001– B 20,000	B20,001– B 25,000	B25,001– B30,000	
Doctor	0.0	0.0	0.0	0.0	100.0	0.0	100.0
Physiotherapist	0.0	62.5	25.0	0.0	0.0	12.5	100.0
Occupational therapist	0.0	50.0	50.0	0.0	0.0	4.5	100.0
Social worker	0.0	50.0	50.0	0.0	0.0	0.0	100.0
Nurse	0.0	16.3	27.8	13.5	25.0	16.7	100.0
Nurse assistant	77.3	13.6	4.5	4.5	0.0	0.0	100.0
Care assistant	82.8	8.6	8.6	0.0	0.0	0.0	100.0
Helper	64.9	5.4	27.0	2.7	0.0	0.0	100.0
Others (admin, staff, chief, laundry, gardeners, drivers)	63.6	9.1	18.2	0.0	4.5	0.0	100.0
Total	52.5 (104)	13.2 (26)	18.3 (36)	3.6 (7)	8.1 (16)	4.1 (8)	100 (197)

B = baht (Thai currency).

Notes:
1. Percentages may not total exactly 100% because of rounding.
2. The numbers in parentheses indicate the actual number of respondents with incomes in each salary range. There were 197 respondents in all.

Source: S. Sasat et al. 2009. *Research Report on Long-Term Care Institutions in Thailand*. Nonthaburi, Thailand: Health Systems Research Institute of Thailand.

3.6.3   Working Conditions and Levels of Satisfaction

There are no official data on working conditions and staff turnover. However, from interviews with owners of private nursing homes and private training schools, researchers have found that there has been a high turnover rate of paid caregivers.[69] There are two reasons why caregivers generally move from one workplace to another: better working conditions and better institutional reputation. For instance, they may move to another facility that has a better working environment, even though the salary is the same. Some became assistants to nurses in hospitals in order to receive better recognition than they would as paid caregivers at someone's home.

The 2009 survey by Sasat et al. also addressed salary satisfaction, and found that most of the care personnel were moderately satisfied with their salaries (55.6%). The percentages were 66.7% for those working in assisted-living facilities, 61.4% of those working in nursing homes, and 56.9% of those working in hospital LTC units (Table 12).

However, 7.1% of the respondents were totally dissatisfied with their salaries. They fell into two groups: 13.2% of those employed in residential homes and 7.7% of those employed in LTC hospitals. Only 1.5% of personnel overall were highly satisfied with their salaries, with the largest contingent comprising 2.3% of those employed in nursing homes. When satisfaction was measured based on occupation, rather than on place of work (Table 13),

---

[69]   S. Sasat et al. 2015. The *Development of Care Standard and Service Guideline for Dependent Older Persons in Long-Term Care Institution in Thailand* [in Thai]. Bangkok.

Table 12: Levels of Satisfaction with Salaries, by Type of Residential Care Facility, 2009
(%)

| Salary Satisfaction Rate | Type of Residential Care Facility | | | | | Total |
	Residential Home	Assisted Living	Hospital LTC Unit	Nursing Home	Hospice Care	
Totally dissatisfied	13.2	0.0	7.7	0.0	0.0	7.1
Dissatisfied	16.2	8.3	6.2	2.3	11.1	9.1
A little satisfied	10.4	16.7	13.8	27.3	33.3	16.7
Moderately satisfied	51.5	66.7	56.9	61.4	33.3	55.6
Very satisfied	7.4	8.3	13.8	6.8	22.2	10.1
Highly satisfied	1.5	0.0	1.5	2.3	0.0	1.5
Total	100.0 (68)	100.0 (12)	100.0 (65)	100.0 (44)	100.0 (9)	100.0 (198)

B = baht (Thai currency), LTC = long-term care.

Notes:

1. Percentages may not total exactly 100% because of rounding.
2. The numbers in parentheses indicate the actual number of respondents working in each type of residential care facility. There were 198 respondents in all.

Source: S. Sasat et al. 2009. *Research Report on Long-Term Care Institutions in Thailand*. Nonthaburi, Thailand: Health Systems Research Institute of Thailand.

Table 13: Levels of Satisfaction with Salaries, by Occupation, 2009
(%)

| Occupation | Salary Satisfaction Rate | | | | | | Total |
	Highly Dissatisfied	Dissatisfied	A Little Satisfied	Moderately Satisfied	Very Satisfied	Highly Satisfied	
Doctors	0.0	0.0	0.0	50.0	33.3	16.7	100.0
Physiotherapists	0.0	12.5	25.0	62.5	0.0	0.0	100.0
Occupational therapists	0.0	0.0	0.0	100.0	0.0	0.0	100.0
Social workers	0.0	0.0	0.0	75.0	25.0	0.0	100.0
Nurses	2.7	5.4	8.1	62.2	21.6	0.0	100.0
Nurse assistants	0.0	0.0	36.4	59.1	4.5	0.0	100.0
Care assistants	8.6	6.9	20.7	56.9	5.2	1.7	100.0
Helpers	10.8	16.2	10.8	54.1	8.1	0.0	100.0
Others (cooks, laundry workers, gardeners, drivers)	18.2	22.7	18.2	27.3	9.1	4.5	100.0

Notes:

1. Percentages may not total exactly 100% because of rounding.

2. The numbers in parentheses indicate the actual number of respondents working in each type of residential care facility. There were 198 respondents in all.

Source: S. Sasat et al. 2009. *Research Report on Long-Term Care Institutions in Thailand*. Nonthaburi, Thailand: Health Systems Research Institute of Thailand.

the study found that 100% of occupational therapists, 75% of social workers, and 62.5% of physiotherapists were moderately satisfied with their salaries. Only a minority of doctors (16.7%) were highly satisfied with their salaries, but they were the largest group in that category. Similarly, only a minority of cooks, laundry workers, gardeners, and drivers were highly dissatisfied with their salaries (18.2%), but they formed the majority of that category.

3.6.4   Staffing and Guidelines

Staffing is an important factor in the quality of care, as insufficient staff can lead to poor care outcomes. There are no official statistics regarding staff-to-patient ratios in Thailand, nor are there guidelines for community and LTC facilities. The only data available on staff-to-patient ratios is from the survey conducted by Sasat et al. in 2009. According to the survey, nursing homes had the highest ratios of nurses to residents (1:5.7) and of physiotherapists to residents (1:31.6). By contrast, residential homes had the lowest ratio of care assistants (1:25.5) and helpers (1:16.2) to residents. Occupational therapists were only found working in nursing homes, where their ratio to residents was 1:47.5, and in assisted-living facilities, where their ratio was 1:130.5 (Table 14).

Table 14: Staff–Older Person Ratios, by Type of Residential Care Facility, 2009

Staff Member	Type of Residential Care Facility				
	Residential Home	Assisted Living	Nursing Home	Long-Term Care Hospital	Hospice Care
Nurse	1:187.3	1:15.3	1:5.7	1:6.2	1:14.8
Practical nurse	1: 2,060.7	1:16.3	1:21.8	1:6.9	1:14.8
Care assistant	1: 25.5	1:6.3	1:1.6	1:2.5	
Helper	1: 16.2		1:142.5		
Physiotherapist	1: 424.8	1:261	1:31.6	1:61.5	1:74.0
Occupational therapist		1:130.5	1:47.5		

Note: Blank spaces represent the absence of the type of staff (represented by the row) at the type of residential care facility (represented by the column).

Source: S. Sasat et al. 2009. *Research Report on Long-Term Care Institutions in Thailand.* Nonthaburi, Thailand: Health Systems Research Institute of Thailand.

Most residential care assistants had been trained in elderly care (68.9%). Among them, the highest number of trained care assistants worked in residential homes, followed by hospitals, hospices, and nursing homes. Of the care assistants working in assisted-living facilities, 60% had never been trained in elderly care (Sasat 2009).

However, there was a frequent lack of professional staff such as nurses, physiotherapists, and occupational therapists, especially in residential homes where more than half of the residents were moderately to totally dependent and in need of a higher level of care (Sasat 2009). In some places, such as Lamsonthi district, the practice was to send physiotherapists and their assistants on home visits after strokes or falls to provide rehabilitation and to teach older persons and/or their family members the recommended exercises.

Standard staff ratios have not been established in Thailand. Referring to international standards, minimum staffing requirements are expressed either in terms of the average number of daily hours of nursing care per patient or in terms of the number of patients each nursing staff member is required to care for (staff-to-patient ratios). For example, in California, the requirement is 3.2 hours per patient per day; this is roughly equivalent to an average ratio of one direct care provider per patient,[70] and per 7.5 patients over the course of a 24-hour period.[71] The federal staffing standards in the United States also include requirements for managerial roles and levels and ratios of nursing staff for nursing homes. An example of proposed minimum staffing ratios for assisted-living facilities and nursing homes in Thailand, classified by profession and the size of institution, is shown in Table 15.

Table 15: Proposed Minimum Staff Ratios, by Type of Institution, Profession, and Size of Institution

Type of Institution/Profession	Number of Staff Members					Proposed Ratio
	Small Institution		Medium-Sized Institution		Large Institution	
	≤10 Beds	11–30 Beds	31–60 Beds	61–90 Beds	91–120 Beds	
Assisted-Living Facility						
Registered nurse	1	1	1	1	1–2	1:100 beds
Physiotherapist/ occupational therapist	1	1	1	1–2	2	1:1–60 beds
Practical nurse	1	1	1	1–2	2	1:1–60 beds
Care assistant/nurse's aide	1	1–2	2–4	4–6	6–8	1:1–15 beds
Nursing Home						
General Practitioner					1	1:100 beds
Registered nurse	1	1	1	1–2	2	1:1–60 beds
Physiotherapist/ occupational therapist	1	1	1	1–2	2	1:1–60 beds
Practical nurse	1	1	1–2	2--3	3–4	1:1–30 beds
Care assistant/nurse's aide	2	2–4	4–8	8-12	12–15	1:1–8 beds

Note: Blank spaces represent the absence of members of the profession (represented by the row) at the type or size of the institution (represented by the column).

Sources: C. Harrington. 2010. Nursing Home Staffing Standards in State Statutes and Regulations. San Francisco: University of California San Francisco, Department of Social and Behavioral Sciences; and S. Sasat, N. Pagaiya, and W. Wisesrith. 2015. *Estimates, Expectations, and Trends in Health Workforce to Support the Aging Society in Thailand.* Nonthaburi, Thailand.

3.6.5   Time Spent in Caring

A study titled "Estimate Time Spent in Caring for Dependent Older People" was conducted in 2013 in a community and in a private nursing home.[72] The study revealed that the average time spent in caring for dependent older persons was almost 8 hours a day, with about 4 hours spent on personal care, 3 hours on social care, and 1 hour on health care (Table 16). More time was spent on care at the nursing home (averaging about 12 hours a day) than in community-based settings (averaging about 4.25 hours). Health personnel provided 1.75 hours of care in community-based care settings, compared with 3.5 hours at the nursing home. Most of the time spent by health

---

[70]   The care provider in this case would be a registered nurse, certified nursing assistant, or licensed vocational nurse.

[71]   State of California, Department of Health Care Services. *A Report to the California Legislature on Nursing Staff Requirements and the Quality of Nursing Home Care.* Sacramento: Department of Health Care Services; and C. Harrington. 2010. Nursing Home Staffing Standards in State Statutes and Regulations. San Francisco: University of California San Francisco, Department of Social and Behavioral Sciences.

[72]   S. Sasat and W. Wisesrith. 2013. *Estimated Time Spent Caring for Dependent Older Persons.* Bangkok.

personnel was in following up on rehabilitation cases at the nursing home. The average time spent on caring was, predictably, affected by the degree of the older person's dependency, with an average of 4 hours for those with moderate care needs, compared with almost 8.5 hours for those with severe care needs.

Table 16: Average Time Spent Caring for Dependent Older Persons, by Type of Activity and Setting, 2013

Caring Activities	In the Community	At the Nursing Home	Average Time for Combined Locations
Health care (e.g., blood sample, rehabilitation, wound dressing, vital signs)	0 h, 36 min	1 h, 36 min	1 h, 4 min
Personal care (e.g., bathing, dressing, cooking)	3 h, 19 min	4 h, 41 min	4 h, 0 min
Social care (e.g., chatting, reading, massaging, cleaning care unit and belongings)	0 h, 21 min	5 h, 39 min	2 h, 51 min
Total average time	4 h, 16 min	11 h, 56 min	7 h, 55 min

h = hour, min = min.

Source: S. Sasat and W. Wisesrith. 2013. *Estimated Time Spent Caring for Dependent Older Persons.* Bangkok.

3.6.6   Training and Qualifications

3.6.6.1   Training of Paid Caregivers and Care Assistants

The training of both paid caregivers and volunteers is usually done via the Care Assistant (Paid Caregivers/Carers) Training Course.

The majority of care assistants are trained by private institutes, with training courses approved by government bodies. The courses are provided for a specified number of hours. Curricula have been developed by three bodies. The Ministry of Education **provides a school-based course** for older persons' paid caregivers and care assistants, but it is also developing **an online course**. School-based training is a 12-week course, or 420 total hours, of which 300 hours are devoted to substantive lectures and 120 hours to practical activities.

The course focuses on the principles of caring for older persons, psychology of old age, activities and recreation for older persons, nutrition for older persons, cleaning and maintenance of household appliances and the home environment, the use of the Thai and English languages, the role and ethics of care assistants or paid caregivers, health education, and the relevant labor laws. There is also an apprenticeship in caring for older persons. In addition, a 2-year diploma course has been developed with approval pending from the Office of the Community College.

The Ministry of Labour's Department of Skills Development has developed a training course, **Care for Children and Older People,** which is a free-of-charge, 60-hour course that enhances the caregiving skills of volunteers and the general public. A minimum practice score of 80% is required prior to taking the achievement test.

The course structure includes basic labor laws, human relationships, communications, principles of caring for children and older persons, personal hygiene, environment and safety in the home, basic needs of older persons, utilization and maintenance of equipment, body cleaning, and caring for older persons. The achievement test includes a 1-hour exam on theory and a 2-hour practical test. **The Ministry of Labour has also prepared a certificate course** in skills development in caring for children and older persons (in preparation for employment), with 6 months (840 hours) of classroom instruction and 2 months (280 hours) of on-the-job training, integrating childcare with LTC for older persons. The course structure includes basic personal care, main and supplementary knowledge, and competency.

The Department of Health, within the Ministry of Public Health (MOPH), has prepared two courses in the care of older persons. The first is a 420-hour training course for care assistants and paid caregivers. Most of the course content is the same as that found in the Ministry of Education's course, but it puts a stronger emphasis on older persons' health. The second is a 70-hour training course initiated by the "Tonkla Archeep" project (part of the government policy of enhancing job and income opportunities, under the economic stimulus package implemented in response to the 2008 global economic crisis). The course content includes basic knowledge and practice, covering the common problems and needs of older persons, first aid, levels of dependency, health promotion, environment management, and recreational activities. People who wish to enroll in this course must have at least 1 year's experience in care provision. Health volunteers or family members of older persons who wish to work as care assistants or paid caregivers must complete this course in accordance with the announcement by the MOPH about businesses that may be harmful to health. This course was also adopted by the pilot project for the Community-Based Long-Term Care Program, under the revised Second National Plan for Older Persons.

3.6.6.2 Home Care Volunteers for the Elderly

The Home Care Volunteers for the Elderly (HCVE) program recruits people from the community who are willing to do volunteer work. Often already working as village health volunteers (VHVs), they must nevertheless attend a 3-day training course organized by the Bureau of Empowerment for Older People, at the Ministry of Social Development and Human Security (MSDHS). The course schedule is as follows: Day One: 7 hours of instruction, including 2 hours on basic older persons' care, 2 hours on the role of the volunteer, and 3 hours on welfare and social services for older persons; Day Two: 5 hours on care and health promotion for older persons; and Day Three: 6 hours on the care and needs of older persons in the community.

3.6.6.3 Caregivers Specializing in Long-Term Care

The 70-hour training course for LTC caregivers, under the government's Community-Based Long-Term Care Program, teaches them to provide quality home health care based an individual care plan, with help from the care manager, and includes sessions in both theory and practice. Among the subjects of instruction are population aging, the need for care, LTC, the rights of older persons, and the role of caregivers (9 hours); common diseases, critical conditions, first aid, care for those with condition-specific challenges, drug administration, health promotion for older persons, and local health wisdom (17 hours); mental health and self-care (5 hours); and home environment and recreation (4 hours). At the end, the students go through work practice, testing, and evaluation (12 hours).[73]

---

[73]   W. Suwanrada et al. 2010. *Long-Term Care System for Old-Age Security Promotion* [in Thai]. Bangkok: Ministry of Social Development and Human Security, Office of the Welfare Promotion Protection and Empowerment of Vulnerable Groups.

3.6.6.4 Care Managers

Care managers also have a 70-hour training course under the Community-Based Long-Term Care Program. The course includes instruction in aging, older persons' rights, the role of a care manager, and basic care management (14 hours); assessment and intake (23 hours); and understanding care delivery (14 hours). It also includes practice sessions (8 hours), study visits, and actual practice at health facilities in the community, as well as practical training and testing (11 hours). See the Appendix for more details on the curriculum content of both the caregiver and care-manager courses.

3.6.6.5 Caregiver Training Courses

There is a 3-day training course (18 hours) for people interested in enhancing their knowledge and capacity to work with older persons in their own families or in their communities. It was initiated by the Institute of Geriatric Medicine, at the Department of Medical Services in the MOPH, and by the Thai Red Cross organization.

Training courses for professional groups are regulated by individual professional councils and the Ministry of Education, so they will not be discussed further in this report. Most nursing programs focus on hospital-based acute care, with no special training in chronic care for dependent older persons. The Department of Older Persons, at the MSDHS, is currently drafting a national, standardized, nonprofessional training curriculum by drawing on the strengths of existing curricula and adding information regarding updated knowledge and new technologies.

3.6.7 Projected Need for Human Resources Capacity

A study titled "Estimates, Expectations, and Trends in Health Workforce to Support the Aging Society in Thailand" was conducted in 2015.[74] The study analyzed the data on older persons, the need for health services at each service level, and the members of the care-provider workforce in each service category. The authors also studied the productivity of each type of worker, and then estimated the demand for care workers.

They found that the LTC workforce demand for older persons in acute-care settings amounted to a further 2,041 doctors, 58,841 nurses, 3,649 physiotherapists, 412 practical nurses, and 82,528 care assistants. The overall shortage of health workers in the medical and public-health service system is well documented, and the increasing demand for LTC workers for older persons would result in worsening shortages in the health workforce.[75] However, there are no current government incentives or support mechanisms to stimulate care service provision by small and medium-sized private care providers. It was recommended that a database be established of service providers and care receivers, and that a workforce specialized in LTC management be developed. Also, the study recommended that the government promote the training of a workforce specialized in LTC services, encourage educational institutions to produce adequate workforce, develop or improve specific courses on LTC, promote holistic and multidisciplinary care, and encourage local experiments to improve the system.

---

[74]   S. Sasat, N. Pagaiya, and W. Wisesrith. 2015. *Estimates, Expectations, and Trends in Health Workforce to Support the Aging Society in Thailand.* Nonthaburi, Thailand; and S. Sasat et al. 2013. Long-Term Care Institutions in Thailand. *Journal of Health Research.* 27 (6). pp. 413–418.

[75]   The Mini-Mental State Examination (MMSE) is a widely used test of cognitive functioning for the elderly. It includes tests of orientation, attention, memory, and language. This tool was translated into Thai and modified by the MOPH. The interpretation of an individual's responses depends on the level of education. Thus, the mental state of uneducated people will be interpreted as normal when they get more than 13 points out of 23. If an older person's education level is primary level, he or she will need to get more than 17 out of 30 points to be designated as normal. However, people who have a level of education higher than primary school will have to get more than 22 out of 30 points to qualify as normal.

Unfortunately, the number of health workers, both professional and nonprofessional, including volunteers, is not yet known. As noted above, volunteers might participate in more than one project or program, so the actual number of volunteers may be overestimated. Moreover, little is known about how many trained caregivers migrate to work overseas or how many foreign caregivers are working in Thailand. A national study on the health workforce is needed to obtain the correct workforce numbers, assist government planning, address shortages of human resources, and to organize human resources development for LTC.

Strategies and initiatives to address shortages in human resources are needed to plan for workforce development. Realistically, most LTC will continue to be provided by family members, so support and training for them would also be a good strategy. For example, the government could consider providing free training and financial assistance for family carers, as they are often prevented by their caregiving responsibilities from earning a sufficient income.

Volunteerism can continue to be part of the solution, through the encouragement of community participation in LTC for older persons. The government emphasizes the importance of volunteer caregivers in delivering LTC services, but it needs to think about how to improve incentives in order to expand and retain the volunteer workforce. Currently, volunteer caregivers receive an allowance of B500 ($16) a month, but this sum should be increased, at least enough to keep up with inflation.

A national standard curriculum and training standards exist for paid caregivers. This is a good start, but it is important to increase the size of the qualified workforce, so measures such as offering loans for training courses and certification, to give the field more legitimacy, would also be useful. If the Ministry of Labour accepts caregiving as a career, it could then set minimum salary standards for the various certification levels, a move that would also help to expand the workforce.

IV. FINANCING LONG-TERM CARE

Thailand joined the ranks of the upper-middle-income countries in 2011, with sustained high growth and rapid poverty reduction.[76] Since 1961, the Thai economy has been transitioning from an agricultural base to a base consisting of services and manufacturing. In 1960, agriculture accounted for 40% of the gross domestic product (GDP), but by 2018 this had decreased to 8%. By contrast, the manufacturing sector's share of GDP rose rapidly from 1980 to 2000 (see Table 17 for some economic indicators). However, economic growth in the country has recently been impeded by global economic shocks, natural disasters, sociopolitical tensions, and relatively low investment. Other challenges to growth include persistent inequality, a weak education system, environmental degradation, and an aging population.[77]

Poverty and inequality remain a challenge for Thailand. Although the poverty rate has mostly declined since the beginning of this century, 9.85% of population (6.7 million) was still considered poor in 2018. In fact, there were about 1.8 million more poor people in 2018 than in 2015. And though inequality has been gradually decreasing, it remains high (footnote 5).

The Thai National Health Accounts (NHA) have been published continuously since 1994. The most recent is NHA 2016, which follows the methodology of the System of Health Accounts 2011.[78] Although the statistical framework for LTC expenditure has already been designed, the NHA's statistics on LTC expenditure may not always be accurate due to problems with data collection.

4.1 Sources of Funding for Long-Term Care

Finance from family members is a major source of funding for LTC in Thailand. Government revenue is a source of finance for the Community-Based Long-Term Care Program, under the National Health Security Office (NHSO). But out-of-pocket payments are the main source of funding for LTC in private residential facilities.

Private nursing homes charge the highest prices for care on average, generally between $102 and $1,780 per month; the next most expensive are the private hospitals, which charge between $373 and $1,627 per month. Public residential homes charge the lowest prices: between $135 and $339 per month.

---

[76] ADB. 2015. *Thailand Industrialization and Economic Catch-Up: Highlights.* ADB Country Diagnostic Studies. Manila. https://www.adb.org/sites/default/files/publication/178077/tha-industrialization-econ-highlights.pdf.

[77] ADB. 2020. *ADB Member Fact Sheet: Thailand.* Manila. https://www.adb.org/sites/default/files/publication/27802/tha-2019.pdf.

[78] Thai National Working Group. 2019. *Thai National Health Accounts 2016.* Nonthaburi, Thailand: International Health Policy Foundation (IHPF) and the NHSO. http://www.ihppthaigov.net/wp-content/uploads/2019/09/NHA-report-2016.pdf.

Table 17: Economic Indicators

GDP 2018 ($)	505 billion
Per capita GDP 2018 ($)	7,445.60
Average wage in 2018 ($ per month)	425.84
National government expenditure in 2018 (% of GDP)	21.2
Local government expenditure in 2018 (% of GDP)	2.6
National government expenditure on social protection, not including health and education, in 2018 (% of GDP)	3.0

GDP = gross domestic product.

Sources: World Bank. DataBank: World Development Indicators. https://databank.worldbank.org/source/world-development-indicators (accessed 9 April 2020); Bank of Thailand. Statistics. https://www.bot.or.th/English/Statistics/Pages/default.aspx (accessed 5 April 2020); Asian Development Bank (ADB). Key Indicators Database. https://kidb.adb.org/kidb/ (accessed 9 April 2020); and Government of Thailand, Ministry of Finance, Fiscal Policy Office. http://www.fpo.go.th/main/Statistic-Database.aspx?fbclid=IwAR1SoC2EibTaMD0ikrb- RtQ7Ua4AH4Sgn8jK3Cq3ZjkFIIP8rEnS-bnRxQ0 (accessed 5 April 2020).

According to the NHA, total public spending on health-related LTC was B1.7 billion in 2012. The MOPH is the major source of finance (B1.6 billion). Spending by nongovernment organizations (NGOs) on health-related LTC was B70.3 million. However, this figure is probably an underestimate, as there is no system for the detailed collection of statistics on LTC activities at public LTC residential facilities under the MSDHS, including the funding from local governments and private sources.

There are also no data available regarding the spending on LTC by social services due to problems with data collection.

4.2 Financial Modeling of Future Needs and Funding

The first attempt to forecast LTC needs in Thailand was done in 2008.[79] Three modeling approaches were used to project the residential LTC needs of older Thai people: a multiple-state model, a modified multiple-state model, and a linear model. The multiple-state model used Australian disability rates, while the modified multiple-state model adjusted the Australian rates to fit the Thai context. The linear model assumed that all the rates would remain constant over time.

The modified multiple-state model estimated that older males with severe and profound dependency would comprise 1.4%–1.9% of all older men during 2004–2024, and that older women with severe and profound dependency would make up 1.7%–2.0% of all older women during the same period. Considering that between 2% and 25% of those with a severe and profound dependency are admitted to residential care, the total costs incurred were predicted to range from B908 million (for 2%) to B11.4 billion (for 25%) in 2009. Given the growing number of older persons, and assuming the same rates of need for—and uptake of—residential care, the total costs were predicted to fall between B2.8 billion (for 2%) and B34.6 billion (for 25%) by 2024.

---

[79] S. Srithamrongsawat and K. Bundhamcharoen. 2010. *Synthesis of Long-Term Care System for the Elderly in Thailand.* Bangkok.

The second projection was carried out in 2013. It was a simple LTC actuarial projection, based on the Rapid Assessment Protocol (RAP),[80] developed with support from French experts and the International Labour Organization (ILO) (footnote 14). The model for this forecast comprised four types of sub-models: the Thai RAP demographic model (called the "POP sheet"); labor market models (EAP and LPR sheets), macroeconomic model (ECO sheet), and general government operations model (GGO sheet) (footnote 28). This projection assumed that all the dependency rates would remain constant over time, and that there would be no changes in the factors influencing care at home (e.g., migration rates and patterns, urbanization, living arrangements, and female workforce participation).

The number of dependent people in each cohort was calculated using the prevalence rate of disability. Then the dependents in each cohort were disaggregated into four groups, based on the level of disability as determined by the Barthel Index (on ADL) and on the level of cognitive functioning as determined by the Mini-Mental State Examination-Thai version (MMSE-T) [Table 18].

Table 18: Categories of Functionality in Activities of Daily Living

Category	ADL (total 100 points)	Severe Cognitive Impairment
Severe group	0–40	Yes
Moderate group	41–74	No
Mild group	75–90	No
Independent group	> 90	No

ADL = activities of daily living.
Source: Government of Thailand, Ministry of Public Health.

The data for this projection came from two available surveys: the 2009–2010 Survey of a Long-Term Care System for Older People's Protection and the 2008–2009 Health Examination Survey of Thailand, which were used to estimate disability prevalence.[81] Both surveys used the Barthel Index and the MMSE-T, and found that the prevalence of disability increased as people aged. The prevalence of disability by level of severity and sex were used to project the number of older persons with disabilities in the future, based on the assumption that the prevalence rates would remain constant during the projection period.

Regarding financial modeling for residential LTC for severe and profound dependency, it was estimated that if the costs incurred were assumed to range in 2009 from B908 million (if 2% of severely and profoundly dependent older adults were admitted for residential LTC) to B11.4 billion (if 25% of such older adults were admitted), the total cost for a 2% admission rate would rise to B2.8 billion by 2024, and that for a 25% admission rate would rise to B34.6 billion (footnote 13).

---

[80] The RAP is a costing tool developed by the ILO. It uses a simple methodology that builds on single-age population projections and single-age estimates of labor force participation rates, along with a relatively simple economic scenario determined by assumptions about overall GDP growth, productivity, inflation, wages, interest rates, and poverty rates. The model uses these variables as drivers of expenditure and revenues, starting from initial statistical values for the last observation years.

[81] *Report on 2009–2010 Survey of a Long-Term Care System for Older People's Protection*. Bangkok; and W. Aekplakorn. 2011. *Thailand National Health Examination Survey 2008–2009* [in Thai]. Nonthaburi, Thailand: National Health Examination Survey of Thailand. https://bit. ly/2RZwqde.

The third estimate focused on community-based LTC. It was a simple actuarial projection done by the Health Insurance System Research Office (HISRO) in 2014 (footnote 75). Using data from 2012, it found that a policy of targeting low-income groups would cost 0.10%–0.56% of government revenue and around 0.02%–0.12% of GDP by 2022. A policy of providing universal coverage of community-based LTC for only severely and profoundly dependent older persons would cost 0.60%–1.10% of government revenue and around 0.16%–0.22% of GDP by the same year (Table 19).

Table 19: Summary of Important Data for the Projection of Long-Term Care by the Health Insurance System Research Office

Statistics Relevant to Long-Term Care	Base Year 2012	Projection Year 2022
Population (number)		
Target population (60+ years of age)	9,122,267	13,605,614
Economic Factors		
GDP at constant price (B million)	4,598,429	7,685,181
GDP at current price (B million)	10,539,446	23,218,781
Government revenue (B million)	2,034,257	5,314,674
Poverty line per month (B)	1,795	2,297
Inflation rate (%)	3	2
Prevalence Rate (%)		
Severely dependent	2.65	2.63
Moderately dependent	1.16	1.15
Dependent Older Persons (number)		
Severely dependent	241,537	358,171
Moderately dependent	106,261	156,392
Take-Up Rate (%)		
Community-Based	90	90
Private Home Care	0	0
Nursing Home	10	10
Aggregate Cost per Year by Dependency Level (B)		
Severely dependent	68,724	110,850
Moderately dependent	50,736	81,836

B = baht (Thai currency), GDP = gross domestic product.

Source: O. Prasitsiriphon et al. 2013. *Costing Model for Long-Term Care System in Thailand*. Bangkok: Health System Research Office.

The HISRO projection included two scenarios of LTC expenditure based on different methods of estimation: the targeting approach (scenario 1) and the universal approach (scenario 2).

Scenario 1 (Table 20) involved targeting with a means test, and three projections were calculated under this scenario. For projection 1, the means test was set at the poverty line; for projection 2, the means test was set at a higher level, which was the poverty line plus 50% of the cost of LTC for severely dependent cases; and for projection 3, the cut-off point of the means test was set at the poverty line plus the full cost of LTC for severely dependent cases. Projection 3 had the means test set at the highest level, and it was based on the cost for the highest number of beneficiaries (0.12% of GDP).

Table 20: Projections of Long-Term Care Expenditure Using the Targeting Approach: Scenario 1

Eligibility and Costs	Base Year 2012	Projection Year 2022
Eligible People under the Three Projections (%)		
Projection 1: income below the poverty line	11	11
Projection 2: income below poverty line + 50% of LTC cost	52	52
Projection 3: income below poverty line + 100% of LTC cost	72	72
Eligible People under the Three Projections (number)		
Projection 1: income below the poverty line	27,047	40,107
Projection 2: income below the poverty line + 50% of LTC cost	125,997	186,838
Projection 3: income below the poverty line + 100% of LTC cost	173,644	257,494
Projection 1: Total Costs		
Total cost (B million)	1,952	4,668
Total cost (% of GDP)	0.02	0.02
Projection 2: Total Costs		
Total cost (B million)	9,092	21,747
Total cost (% of GDP)	0.08	0.09
Projection 3: Total Costs		
Total cost (B million)	12,530	29,970
Total cost (% of GDP)	0.11	0.12

B = baht (Thai currency), GDP = gross domestic product.

Source: O. Prasitsiriphon et al. 2013. *Costing Model for Long-Term Care System in Thailand.* Bangkok: Health System Research Office.

As mentioned scenario 2 under this model was based on the universal approach. The scenario generated two figures, one showing the LTC expenditure for only the severely dependent group (scenario 2.1, Table 21), and the other showing the LTC expenditure for the moderately and severely dependent groups combined (scenario 2.2, Table 22).

As part of the universal approach, a sensitivity analysis was carried out using three levels of wages paid to caregivers under both scenario 2.1 and scenario 2.2. The first level was a wage of B5,000 per month during the baseline year (2012), in a rural area. The second level was the official minimum wage, B7,620 per month; and the third level was the market rate for caregivers, B12,000 per month. The total expenditure for the severely dependent group was 0.78%–2.25% of government revenue and around 0.16%–0.47% of GDP. When coverage is expanded to include the moderately dependent level, expenditure increased to 1.40%–3.50% of government revenue and 0.20%–0.74% of GDP by 2022.

Table 21: Projection for Long-Term Care Expenditure Using the Universal Approach: Scenario 2.1

Costs for the Severely Dependent	Base Year 2012	Projection Year 2022
Total Costs		
Total cost (B million)	17,429	41,688
Total costs (% of GDP)	0.16	0.17
Total Costs at Various Wage Levels		
B7,620 per Month		
Total cost (B million)	28,784	77,981
Total cost (% of GDP)	0.26	0.31
B9,000 per Month		
Total cost (B million)	32,343	88,148
Total cost (% of GDP)	0.29	0.35
B12,000 per Month		
Total cost (B million)	40,081	110,252
Total cost (% of GDP)	0.36	0.44

B = baht (Thai currency), GDP = gross domestic product.

Source: O. Prasitsiriphon et al. 2013. *Costing Model for Long-Term Care System in Thailand.* Bangkok: Health System Research Office.

Table 22: Projection for Long-Term Care Expenditure Using the Universal Approach: Scenario 2.2

Costs for the Moderately and Severely Dependent	Base Year 2012	Projection Year 2022
Total Costs		
Total cost (B million)	23,090	55,127
Total costs (% of GDP)	0.21	0.22
Total Costs at Various Wage Levels		
B7,620 per Month		
Total cost (B million)	44,180	120,344
Total cost (% of GDP)	0.39	0.48
B9,000 per Month		
Total cost (B million)	49,921	136,744
Total cost (% of GDP)	0.45	0.54
B12,000 per Month		
Total cost (B million)	62,402	172,398
Total cost (% of GDP)	0.56	0.68

B = baht (Thai currency), GDP = gross domestic product.

Source: O. Prasitsiriphon et al. 2013. *Costing Model for Long-Term Care System in Thailand.* Bangkok: Health System Research Office.

V. DISCUSSION AND COMMENTARY

5.1 Limitations of Findings and Gaps in Information

While Thailand has more research data available than many other low- and middle-income countries in the region, the lack of useful statistics on LTC was still a key limitation of this study. No well-designed study has been done on the prevalence of LTC need. There are no accurate statistics for the number of residential LTC institutions, and human resources for LTC are underestimated due to a lack of official administrative registration. Data on expenditure, which was collected in the National Health Accounts (NHA), is also underestimated. Further data are needed for recalculation.

There is no LTC information system in Thailand, and there is insufficient data on LTC. Data are needed on the supply side, in areas such as LTC providers, human resources, and particularly care assistants working in older persons' homes or in LTC facilities. As for the prevalence of moderate and severe dependency in older persons, unit cost is a necessary statistic on the demand side.

5.2 The Current Debate on Long-Term Care Reform

5.2.1 Human Resources Development

The shortage of human resources in health care in Thailand is well known. The need for sufficient human resources for LTC puts additional pressure on an already-stretched health workforce. A long-term workforce plan will be needed to ensure that sufficient human resources are generated to care for the growing population of older persons with care needs.[82]

To improve the quality of LTC, an appropriate design for the care workforce is essential. LTC is a new approach in Thailand. The majority of health professionals have been trained in acute-care settings, so their LTC knowledge and skills are limited. Capacity building is needed for both the professional and nonprofessional members of the care workforce. A standard training curriculum for LTC at each level of care, each level of need, and across each professional discipline is also necessary, based on each discipline's professional competencies.

The Department of Older Persons, at the MSDHS, is drafting a standardized nonprofessional training curriculum on caring for older persons. As part of that process, it is gathering all available curricula

---

[82] S. Sasat et al. 2013. Long-Term Care Institutions in Thailand. *Journal of Health Research*. 27 (6). pp. 413–418.

developed by different organizations. The new standard curriculum will draw on the strengths of the existing curricula, and add further information based on recently generated knowledge and new technologies.

5.2.2   Quality of Care

The Acts on the Elderly of 2003 and 2010 held that the quality of care for older persons needed to be improved, and focus group participants have concurred that care standards are essential for improving the quality of life for residents of care homes. The Department of Health Service Support (DHSS), within the Ministry of Public Health (MOPH), has started drafting national standards for LTC facilities. These standards will include research findings, as well as the opinions and views of key stakeholders, including the MOPH, the MSDHS, private care providers, care receivers, and nongovernment organizations (NGOs). The Department of Older Persons has called for cooperation from all stakeholders in the drafting of an integrated health- and social-care standard for curricula and training, standards for nonprofessional care providers, and standards for the buildings and the environments of LTC facilities. However, the lack of a legal framework, particularly for LTC facilities, has slowed down this initiative. Also needed is an LTC accreditation process for care providers at all levels, as well as certification for human resources.

5.2.3   Policy and Regulatory Framework

The legal framework, policies, and governance regarding older persons' LTC in Thailand are fragmented. A specific legal framework or coordination mechanism for public community-based LTC is needed. There are overlaps in the current legal framework of different laws on private facilities, such as the Sanatorium Act B.E. 2541 (1998), the Health Establishment Act B.E. 2559 (2015), Acts on the Elderly B.E. 2546 (2003) and B.E. 2553 (2010), and the Determining Plans and Process of Decentralization Act B.E. 2542 (1999).

Specific LTC legislation is needed that would include regulation, registration, certification, and inspection for both home care and residential care services. The Department of Older Persons should introduce this legislation; the Department of Service Support, under the Ministry of Public Health (MOPH), has a mandate to register and regulate private health enterprises, including LTC service providers.

Current regulations requiring new buildings to be accessible to persons with disabilities, enacted in 2005, do not cover every type of building, or old buildings. A 2015 age-friendliness assessment of public buildings found that many government offices, department stores, and temples were not age-friendly.[83]

5.2.4   Financing of Care

The main sources for the carers of dependent older persons are the older persons' families and volunteers. While these carers are not paid, it is important to recognize their contributions to the care economy.

The financing of a universal, community-based LTC system is being debated, with LTC currently financed through both health and social services. The financing of health-oriented LTC is part of the Universal Coverage Scheme (UCS), which itself is a keenly debated topic, given that the scheme is 100% tax financed, without a cost-sharing mechanism. Measures to improve UCS efficiency and cost containment are under consideration, as is the need to find new sources of finance and new ways to raise taxes. Initial studies on the feasibility of LTC insurance are being conducted. In relation to the financing of LTC focused on social support, local authorities will need

---

[83]   Government of Thailand, National Reform Council of Thailand. 2015. *Reform Agenda No. 30: Reform System for Mitigation of Aging Society* [in Thai]. Bangkok.

to amend their regulations before they can finance these activities. Projections clearly show that new financing sources will be needed, including local taxes or tax transfers.

Public financing or provision of residential LTC is not on the current policy agenda. Instead, the main focus is on housing for active older persons using private funds. Public support for housing is only for vulnerable groups. However, care services are needed by those who live in public residential homes. Demand for residential nursing care homes is likely to rise, particularly for those with 24-hour care and complex health and care services. Older adults who live alone and/or without much informal support are likely to need residential LTC with lower levels of care support, unless home- and community-based care provision significantly increases in scope.

Given that the public provision of residential LTC is unlikely, some of the demand may be met by private LTC homes with public financing for a number of specific places, as needed. Ensuring adherence to the basic standards laid out in the Health Establishment Act B.E. 2559 (2015) may be a useful step toward stimulating the development of quality private LTC facilities. One option would be to consider soft loans to private LTC facilities for capital investment to adhere to official standards and practices.

Older persons and their families will also need financial mechanisms to help them manage their income and share the risk, in order to avoid catastrophic LTC expenditure. A government subsidy is another potential source of finance for older persons' catastrophic LTC support, but this option requires further discussion.

The capacity to design and implement LTC financing through methods such as reverse mortgages and LTC insurance is also limited. Although there are resource people in Thai academic institutions, some technical areas may need experts from other countries who have already gained the relevant implementation experience. Focus group discussions and in-depth interviews conducted by the Ministry of Finance (MOF) and the Office of Insurance Commission (OIC) have identified the gaps in the country's capacity to design, implement, and monitor the technical aspects of LTC-related initiatives.

Reverse mortgages will be promoted as an option, and the Government Savings Bank plans to provide such mortgages. However, the market for secondhand houses in Thailand is not functioning well, so this financial instrument might not be suitable for Thailand at this stage. A lack of data on morbidity rates also presents a challenge to the design of reverse mortgage products.

There is also no private LTC insurance scheme in Thailand. The OIC plans to initiate one in view of the aging of Thai society. However, product design and capacity building are needed for both the OIC and private insurers.

VI. CONCLUSIONS AND PRIORITY RECOMMENDATIONS

6.1 Conclusions

This country diagnostic study has shown that Thailand has been relatively proactive in progressing with LTC system development that is based on available evidence and informed by the best international practices. The emphasis on aging in place and investment in piloting, evaluating, and expanding integrated, community-based home care programs, as well as on nurturing the volunteer workforce, constitutes a reasonable approach, given the context and need. More support for family and other informal carers is recommended, including financial support, insurance, and other risk-pooling strategies. Further development of community-based care services—such as community day care, respite care, and specialist services—would also help to ensure that care needs are met, particularly as family sizes continue to shrink and the population of those with care needs continues to grow. Work on improving the various elements of the LTC system—including policy frameworks, governance, service provision, human resources, management, and financing—should continue, in order to make LTC sustainable and affordable for the government and for patients and their families.

Other systems that need to be integrated with LTC must also be improved. Most notably, these include (i) the health system, including services such as specialist care, rehabilitation services, primary health care, and geriatric medicine; (ii) the social protection system, including disability and social pension allowances, health insurance, and, perhaps eventually, LTC insurance; and (iii) age-friendly communities and supportive environments. Person-centered care should be promoted, and care planning should encourage the full engagement of the individual receiving the care.

6.2 Priority Recommendations

6.2.1 A Supportive Environment, Health Services, and Social Services in Support of a Long-Term Care System for Older Persons

(i) A system design for the implementation of LTC is needed—specifically, one that strikes a balance between community-based LTC and residential LTC, and between the public and private sectors. The care needs of various groups must be met, including those of older persons living in public residential homes; moderately and severely dependent older persons living at home, whether alone or with others; and older persons living in nursing homes.

(ii) A housing and supportive-environment policy for an aging society should encourage people to spend their later years at home.

(iii) The government should clarify how senior living complexes will be managed and overseen. Roles for local and national governments, the private sector, and civil society should be clearly defined and communicated.

(iv)   Increased demand for senior living complexes is attracting investment. The government should ensure that the investment environment remains attractive and is not overly regulated, but also ensure that minimum standards are in place.

(v)   The concepts of an age-friendly environment and "aging in place" should drive the design of low- and middle-income public housing.

(vi)   Appropriate private and public residential LTC facilities should be established in Thailand.

(vii)   The government should establish clear standards and regulations for the operation of all residential facilities (e.g., living complexes, residential homes) that are agreed to by all stakeholders. It should also ensure that these standards and regulations are communicated clearly to all the stakeholders.

(viii)   Local administration organizations (LAOs) should be empowered to establish and manage community day care centers.

6.2.2   Governance and Coordination

(i)   LAOs should be empowered to manage care for older persons, including LTC-related and age-friendly modifications.

(ii)   A national mechanism should be established for the coordination and integration of LTC planning and monitoring, involving ministries, the auditor general, local authorities, and civil society.

(iii)   Current regulations should be updated and improved to ensure disabled-accessible buildings, including older buildings that need retrofitting.

(iv)   Standards should be established and implemented for age-friendly public transportation, using design-for-all standards.

(v)   Legal frameworks should be strengthened to ensure that older persons with disabilities or dementia have legal access to guardians for their protection.

6.2.3   Financing Long-Term Care

(i)   The development of an improved actuarial model is needed for LTC services; it should account for all sources of finance and cover community-based and residential LTC, both public and private.

(ii)   LTC insurance is necessary, but the system design and benefits package should be developed carefully. Private LTC insurance should be an add-on, on top of insurance covering public community-based LTC. Private insurers should work together and establish a pooling fund because if they stand alone, they will be at a high risk for heavy financial loss.

(iii)   Financing for residential LTC must involve the coordination of related ministries. Private financing tools such as reverse mortgages linked with LTC insurance should be explored, and a government subsidy for poor older persons needs more discussion.

(iv)   The OIC should be made the focal point for the preparation of a statistical framework for standard private LTC insurance policies. A risk-pooling mechanism or national-level reinsurance mechanism is also needed.

(v)   There should be an investment in advocacy and training curricula for policy makers, financial analysts, and the staff of relevant ministries, so they can plan projects concerning older persons' care more effectively, including senior living complexes.

6.2.4　Registration and Care Standards for Long-Term Care Establishments

(i)　Care standards are urgently needed for community-based LTC because, for the foreseeable future, the vast majority of dependent older persons will be looked after in their communities. Care standards and service guidelines for dependent older persons in LTC establishments need reviewing, as present standards are not specific to LTC.

(ii)　The establishment of a regulatory mechanism for ensuring a high quality of service and the protection of older persons' rights and dignity is a priority.

(iii)　The establishment of standards may be gradual, using a stepped approach toward achieving a high standard of quality. Providers should be actively involved in the process of developing standards to ensure these standards are applicable in practice.

(iv)　Decentralization needs to go a step further, so that local authorities can be empowered to regulate LTC systems; LAOs should be empowered to take on a role of regulation of care services.

6.2.5　Human Resources Development

(i)　Systematic plans are needed for recruitment processes, standardized curricula, training methods, and registration for human resources, and for the future introduction of accreditation and certification requirements.

(ii)　Those needing training in LTC are a very varied group. Training should be opened up, where possible, to enable informal caregivers, volunteers, and paid caregivers to interact with each other and benefit from each other's skills and knowledge regarding the LTC needs of older persons.

6.2.6　Improvement of Long-Term Care Service in Homes and Residential Facilities

(i)　Specific LTC legislation is needed to improve the quality of LTC at the homes of dependent older persons and in the various types of residential facilities. This legislation may include regulations, registration and certification requirements, and inspections of both home care and residential care services.

(ii)　A statistics and information system on LTC should be established.

(iii)　A committee or task force with representation from the relevant ministries and other stakeholders should be established to review the current statistics and information systems regarding LTC. The committee or task force should then assign or establish an official coordination body, which would be responsible for setting up standards for statistics and information systems regarding LTC.

APPENDIX

CAPACITY DEVELOPMENT CURRICULA FOR CARE MANAGERS AND CAREGIVERS

	Care Manager	
Lesson Plans	Topics	Allotted Time (hours)
Lesson Plan 1	Aging Society and Connected Issues	2
Lesson Plan 2	Basic Principles of Nursing Care Management (care management)	2
Lesson Plan 3	Work Procedures (care management)	2
Lesson Plan 4	Social Resources for Management and How to Utilize Them (care management)	2
Lesson Plan 5	Techniques of Interviewing in the System (care management)	4
Lesson Plan 6	Identifying Target People to Assist Them and Acknowledge Their Problems	2
Lesson Plan 7	Intake Work (receiving and screening of incident reports, and preparations for dealing with situations)	1
Lesson Plan 8	Understanding the Assessment	2
Lesson Plan 9	Conducting an Assessment Based on the International Classification of Functioning, Disabilities, and Health (ICF)	4
Lesson Plan 10	Typology of Aged (TAI) with Illustrations	14
Lesson Plan 11	Practical Session Based on a Case Study	1
Lesson Plan 12	Understanding the Issues Related to Older People and the Procedures to Be Taken in Providing Assistance	14
Lesson Plan 13	Practical Session based on Case Study Involving Relevant Issues	7
Lesson Plan 14	Rights of Older People as Provided in Constitution; Interesting and Relevant Laws	1
Lesson Plan 15	Roles and Ethics of the Care Manager	1
Lesson Plan 16	Study Visit and Practice at Health Facilities and in the Community	3.5+3.5
Lesson Plan 17	Testing and Evaluation of the Training	4
	Total	70

Caregiver		
Lesson Plans	Topics	Allotted Time (hours)
Lesson Plan 1	The Need for Older People's Care (theory)	1
Lesson Plan 2	Concept of an Aging Population (theory)	1
Lesson Plan 3	Common Diseases in Older People (theory: 2 hours; practice session: 1 hour)	3
Lesson Plan 4	Critical Conditions and First-Aid Procedures (theory: 2 hours; practice session: 2 hours)	4
Lesson Plan 5	Introduction to Long-Term Care (theory: 3 hours; practice session: 2 hours)	5
Lesson Plan 6	Care of Dependent Elders with Feeding Problems; the Problems of Respiratory, Eliminatory, and Reproductive Systems	1+2
Lesson Plan 7	Drug Administration for Older People (theory)	2
Lesson Plan 8	Health Promotion for Older People	2+1
Lesson Plan 9	Mental Health and Older People: Self-Care to Relieve Stress (theory: 3 hours; practice session: 2 hours)	5
Lesson Plan 10	Arrangement of an Appropriate Environment (theory)	1
Lesson Plan 11	Local Wisdom and Health Care for Older People (theory: 1 hour; practice session: 1 hour)	2
Lesson Plan 12	Rights of Older People as Provided by the Constitution; Interesting and Relevant Laws (theory)	1
Lesson Plan 13	Roles and Ethics of Caregivers (theory)	1
Lesson Plan 14	Organizing Recreational Activity for Older People (theory: 1 hour; practice session: 1 hour)	2
Lesson Plan 15	Work Practice Session	10
Lesson Plan 16	Testing and Evaluation of the Training (theory: 1 hour; practice session: 1 hour)	1+1
	Total	70 hours

Note: In the "Allotted Time" columns in the Care Managers and Caregivers sections, where there are two numbers separated by a "+" sign, the lesson is broken up into separate sessions, with the numbers indicating the length of each session.

Source: National Health Security Office (NHSO). 2016. *Manual of Guidelines to Support the Management of Long-Term Care Services for Dependent Elders in the Universal Health Security Scheme.* Bangkok.

GLOSSARY

The terms below have been adapted from a number of sources. Those which are directly taken from the *World Report on Ageing and Health*, published by the World Health Organization (WHO) in 2015, are referenced as "WHO 2015."

accessibility	Describes the degree to which an environment, service, or product allows access by as many people as possible (WHO 2015).
activities of daily living (ADL)	The basic activities necessary for daily life, such as bathing or showering, dressing, eating, getting in or out of bed or chairs, using the toilet, and getting around inside the home (WHO 2015).
adult day care	Medical or nonmedical care on a less than 24-hour basis, for persons in need of personal services, supervision, protection, or assistance in sustaining daily needs, including eating, bathing, dressing, ambulating, transferring, toileting, and taking medications (California Code Insurance Code, 2018, Section 10232.9.)
aging in place	Supporting older persons to live in their homes and communities safely, comfortably, and independently.
Alzheimer's disease	The most common cause of dementia. It destroys brain cells and nerves disrupting the transmitters that carry messages in the brain, particularly those responsible for storing memories (Alzheimer's Disease International. Alzheimer's disease.) See: dementia
assessment	A systematic process to collect information on care needs of older persons, based on a set of predefined concepts and data categorization to guide care planning. Clinicians or trained professionals typically use assessment to evaluate the physical, cognitive, and functional care needs of older persons and rank their levels of impairment (OECD/European Union. 2013. *A Good Life in Old Age? Monitoring and Improving Quality in Long-term Care.*) See: comprehensive assessment

assisted living	Accommodation for adults who can live independently but require regular help with some daily activities: hospitality services, personal care, home care. Usually available through subsidized or private-pay operators. Alternatives: extra-care housing
assistive technology (or assistive devices)	Any device designed, made, or adapted to help a person perform a particular task; products may be generally available or specially designed for people with specific losses of capacity; assistive health technology is a subset of assistive technologies, the primary purpose of which is to maintain or improve an individual's functioning and well-being (WHO 2015).
care coordination	The provision of care that coordinates various services around an individual. Typically, it involves a "care coordinator" who ensures goals agreed with the individual are achieved through effective delivery of care by appropriate agencies. Care coordination is most appropriate for older persons who are supported by a high number of different agencies, or who have complex needs. See: integrated care
care services	Services provided by others to meet care needs.
care setting	The place where users of care services live, such as in the home and the community, nursing home, assisted-living facilities/sheltered housing or private homes, care at home and in the community.
caregiver	A person who provides care and support to someone else; such support may include • helping with self-care, household tasks, mobility, social participation, and meaningful activities; • offering information, advice, and emotional support, as well as engaging in advocacy, providing support for decision-making and peer support, and helping with advance care planning; • offering respite services; and • engaging in activities to improve the patient's intrinsic capacity. Caregivers may include family members, friends, neighbors, volunteers, care workers, and health professionals (WHO 2015).
case management	Collaborative process of assessment, planning, facilitation, care coordination, evaluation, and advocacy for options and services to meet an individual's and family's comprehensive health needs (Case Management Society of America. *What Is A Case Manager?*) See: integrated care

catastrophic expenditure	A term used to describe high levels of out-of-pocket expenditure on essential services (e.g., health and social care).
community care	Services and support to help people with care needs to live as independently as possible in their communities (Better Health Channel. Carer Services and Support.)
complex care	Complex care requires a higher level of personal assistance often requiring 24-hour supervision, personal nursing care, and/or treatment by skilled nursing staff (Government of British Columbia. Long-Term Care Services.)
comprehensive assessment (CA)	A multidimensional process that incorporates an in-depth assessment of a person's physical, medical, psychological, cultural, and social needs, capabilities and resources, and is inclusive of carers (Victoria State Government. Assessment Process.)
compression of morbidity theory	Conceptualized by James Fries. The theory that increasing longevity can be accompanied by shorter periods of chronic disease and disability. Under this theory, people live longer and healthier lives (J. Fries. 2003. Measuring and Monitoring Success in Compressing Morbidity. *Annals of Internal Medicine*. pp. 139, 455–459.)
dementia	A loss of brain function that affects mental function related to memory impairment, low level of consciousness and executive function. The most common form of dementia is Alzheimer's disease (National Institute on Aging. What Is Dementia? Symptoms, Types, and Diagnosis.)
demographic dividend	Refers to a period—usually 20–30 years—when fertility rates fall due to significant reductions in child and infant mortality rates. The proportion of nonproductive dependents reduces and is often accompanied by an extension in average life expectancy that increases the portion of the population that is in the working-age group (A. A. M. Shohag. 2015. Demographic Dividend: Reality and Possibility for Bangladesh. *The Independent*. 22 August.)
dependency	The need for frequent human help or care beyond that habitually required by a healthy adult. Alternatively, the inability to perform one or more activities of daily living and instrumental activities of daily living without help (Alzheimer's Disease International. 2013. *World Alzheimer Report 2013. Journey of Caring: An Analysis of Long-Term Care for Dementia.*) Disability may be a cause of dependency, but many disabilities can be managed without frequent human help. Dependency can be categorized on a scale or in categories with a very small amount of people being considered totally dependent.

dependency ratio	The ratio of dependent people (older persons and children) to working-age people (aged 15–64). May be split into old-age dependency ratios and child dependency ratios (B. Mirkin and M. B. Weinberger. 2001. *The Demography of Population Ageing.*)
disability	Disability is an umbrella term, covering impairments, activity limitations, and participation restrictions. An impairment is a problem in body function or structure; an activity limitation is a difficulty encountered by an individual in executing a task or action; while a participation restriction is a problem experienced by an individual in involvement in life situations (WHO definition).
eligibility	Entitlement of an individual to access the programs or services funded directly or indirectly by the government. Often determined on the basis of income or severity of dependency.
environment	All the factors in the extrinsic world that form the context of an individual's life; these include home, communities, and the broader society; within these environments are a range of factors, including the built environment, people and their relationships, attitudes and values, health and social policies, and systems and services (WHO 2015).
environmental hazards	Hazards associated with one's living environment, in and outside the home. Hazards may be objective (real, observable) e.g., lack of electricity; or subjective (simply based on perception) e.g., anticipation of risk such as high crime rate in the neighborhood.
evidence based	Professional practice that is based on a theoretical body of knowledge, empirically evaluated, and is known to be beneficial and effective for the client.
filial piety	The virtue of respect for one's father, elders, and ancestors. In the care context, it relates to the obligation of children to care for their parents, directly and indirectly (through material means).
formal care	The divide between formal and informal care differs between countries. Generally it is determined based on whether the individuals providing care are paid or unpaid, trained or untrained, and/or organized or unorganized. Formal care can take place in the home (home help, home care, home nursing), the community (adult day care, respite care), or in residential care (nursing home, residential care home, hospice care). See: informal care
functional ability	The health-related attributes that enable people to be and to do what they have reason to value; it is made up of the intrinsic capacity of the individual, relevant environmental characteristics, and the interactions between the individual and these characteristics (WHO 2015).

functioning	An umbrella term for body functions, body structures, activities, and participation; it denotes the positive aspects of the interaction between an individual (with a health condition) and that individual's contextual factors (environmental and personal factors) (WHO 2015).
health literacy	The skills and information to allow people to better manage and improve their health.
healthy aging	The development and maintenance of optimal mental, social, and physical well-being and function in older adults. This is most likely to be achieved when communities are safe, promote health and well-being, and use health services and community programs to prevent or minimize disease (New Mexico Department of Health. *Healthy Aging.*) Alternatives: active aging
healthy life expectancy	The average number of years that a person can expect to live in "full health," excluding the years lived in less than full health due to disease and/or injury (WHO definition).
home- and community-based care	Services that support older persons continue to live in their own homes and communities (National Institute on Aging. *Aging in Place: Growing Older at Home.*) See: aging in place
home care	Help with personal care (see activities of daily living) and basic household tasks (see instrumental activities of daily living) such as light housekeeping, laundry, basic shopping, meal preparation, household management; and reminders for personal care and medication (Joint Commission Resources and Joint Commission on Accreditation Health. 2012. *Standards for Home Health, Personal Care and Support Services, and Hospice: 2012.* Illinois: Joint Commission Resources. p. 168.) Alternatives: domiciliary care or home help (usually involves less personal care)
hospitality services	Refers to services such as meal services, housekeeping services, laundry services, social and recreational opportunities, and a 24-hour emergency response system (The Community Care and Assisted Living Act of Canada. 2002. Definition.)
impairment	A loss or abnormality in body structure or physiological function (including mental functions); in this report, abnormality is used strictly to refer to a significant variation from established statistical norms (that is, deviation from a population mean within measured standard norms) (WHO 2015). See: disability

independent living	Housing for seniors that may or may not provide hospitality services. In this living arrangement, seniors lead an independent lifestyle that requires minimal or no extra assistance (J. R. Pratt. 2016. *Long-Term Care: Managing Across the Continuum.* 4th ed. MA: Burlington. p. 180.)
informal care	Care provided by spouses and partners; other members of the household; and other relatives, friends, and neighbors. Informal care is usually provided at home and is typically unpaid and not part of an organized service delivery system (OECD. 2005. *Long-term Care for Older People.*) See: formal care
institutional care	Long-term residential care provided within an institutional setting, usually a nursing home, care home, or, less commonly, a hospital or hospice. Institutional care comprises 24-hour care and accommodation and may include the provision of meals, personal care and supervision, and nursing care (OECD. 2007. *Health at a Glance 2007, OECD Indicators.*)
instrumental activities of daily living (IADL)	Activities that support independence but are not fundamental to survival; including housework, meal preparation, shopping, accounting, medication management, and transportation.
integrated care	A concept bringing together inputs, delivery, management, and organization of services related to diagnosis, treatment, care, rehabilitation, and health promotion. Reflects a concern to improve patient experience and achieve greater efficiency and value from health delivery systems (O. Groene and M. Garcia-Barbero. 2001. Integrated Care: A Position Paper of the WHO European Office for Integrated Health Care Services. *International Journal of Integrated Care.* 1 June.) See: care coordination
international classification of functioning, disability, and health	A classification of health and health-related domains that describe body functions and structures, activities, and participation; the domains are classified from different perspectives: body, individual, and societal; because an individual's functioning and disability occur within a context, this classification includes a list of environmental factors (WHO 2015).
intrinsic capacity	The composite of all the physical and mental capacities that an individual can draw on (WHO 2015).
long-term care	As defined by WHO in the World Report on Ageing and Health (2015): Long-term care is "the activities undertaken by others to ensure that people with or at risk of a significant ongoing loss of intrinsic capacity can maintain a level of functional ability consistent with their basic rights, fundamental freedoms and human dignity."

out-of-pocket expenditure	Payments for goods or services that include (i) direct payments, such as payments for goods or services that are not covered by any form of insurance; (ii) cost sharing, which is a provision of health insurance or third-party payment that requires the individual who is covered to pay part of the cost of the health care received; and (iii) informal payments, such as unofficial payments for goods and services, that should be fully funded from pooled revenue (WHO 2015).
palliative care	An approach that improves the quality of life of patients and their families facing the problem associated with life-threatening illness, through the prevention and relief of suffering by means of early identification and impeccable assessment and treatment of pain and other problems, physical, psychosocial, and spiritual (WHO definition).
pay-as-you-go	A financing model where contributions (through social insurance or specific tax) are collected and then used to pay for current expenditure rather than saved for future expenditure (i.e., not fully funded schemes).
person-centered approach	An approach to care that consciously adopts the perspectives of individuals, families, and communities, and sees them as participants as well as beneficiaries of health care and long-term care systems that respond to their needs and preferences in humane and holistic ways; ensuring that people-centered care is delivered requires that people have the education and support they need to make decisions and participate in their own care; it is organized around the health needs and expectations of people rather than diseases (WHO 2015).
personal care	Assistance that helps an older person to remain independent. May be provided formally or informally and may be related to (iv) activities of daily living; eating, mobility, dressing, grooming, bathing, or personal hygiene; (v) medication; distribution of medication, administration of medication, or monitoring of medication use; (vi) maintenance or management of the cash resources or other properties of a resident or person in care; or (vii) monitoring of food intake or of adherence to therapeutic diets. (The Community Care and Assisted Living Act of Canada. 2002. Definition.) Alternative: personal assistance
private-pay	Services that are paid for completely by elderly care service users.
public–private partnership	A government service or private business venture that is funded and operated through a partnership of government and one or more private sector companies (U. Sawhney. 2014. Chapter 9: Public Private Partnership for Infrastructure Development: A Case of Indian Punjab. In U. Hacioğlu and H. Dinçer. *Globalization and Governance in the International Political Economy*. Panjab University, Chandigarh, India.)

publicly subsidized	Service users with higher incomes pay up to a maximum amount based on comparable private services. Service users who receive income assistance may pay a predetermined set rate (Government of British Columbia. *Publicly Subsidized or Private Pay Services.*)
rehabilitation	A set of measures aimed at individuals who have experienced or are likely to experience disability to assist them in achieving and maintaining optimal functioning when interacting with their environments (WHO 2015).
residential care	Refers to a wide range of housing options aimed at older persons; including nursing and care facilities (other than hospitals) and senior housing. Typically for older persons with care needs who require frequent personal care or close access to support.
	In some countries, the term residential care is used to cover institutions that essentially provide shelter to people without the economic means or family support to live independently.
	See: assisted living
resilience	The ability to maintain or improve a level of functional ability in the face of adversity through resistance, recovery, or adaptation (WHO 2015).
self-care (or self-management)	Activities carried out by individuals to promote, maintain, treat, and care for themselves, as well as to engage in making decisions about their health (WHO 2015).
social care	Assistance with the activities of daily living (such as personal care, maintaining the home) (WHO 2015).
social pension	Noncontributory cash income given to older persons by the government. May be universal (cash income given to all older persons, regardless of their socioeconomic status) or means-tested (solely for the poor and are conditional on the level of income). Some countries use alternate terms such as "old age allowance" or "social assistance," reserving the term "pension" for civil servant pensions and contributory schemes.
transitional care	Refers to the coordination and continuity of care during a movement from one care setting to another or to the home.
universal design	Broad-spectrum ideas for producing buildings, products, and environments that are inherently accessible to older persons, and to people with and without disabilities. Principles of universal designs are equitable use, flexibility in use, simple and intuitive, perceptible information, tolerance for error, low physical effort, and size and space for approach and use (National Disability Authority. *What is Universal Design.*)
	Alternative: inclusive design

REFERENCES

Aekplakorn, W. 2009. *Report on the Fourth National Health Examination Survey: 2008–2009*. Bangkok: National Health Security Office.

———. 2011. Thailand National Health Examination Survey 2008–2009 [in Thai]. Nonthaburi, Thailand: National Health Examination Survey of Thailand. https://bit.ly/2RZwqde.

———. 2014. Report on the Fifth National Health Examination Survey: 2013–2014. Nonthaburi, Thailand: National Health Examination Security Office.

Amorim, A., and Hoang Viet Tran, eds. 2018. South–South and Triangular Cooperation and the Care Economy: A compilation of short South–South Cooperation articles for the Expert Meeting on Future of Work in Asia: "Skills Development Strategies to Promote Employment-Rich and Equitable Growth in the Care Economy." Geneva: International Labour Organization.

Asian Development Bank (ADB). 2016. Technical Assistance for Strengthening Developing Member Countries' Capacity in Elderly Care. Manila.

Chapon, P.-M., coordinator, and E. Rosenberg, translator. 2013. Adapting Cities to Aging: Issues of Development and Governance. Paris: Center for Strategic Analysis.

Charuthat, T. 2005. Minimum Standards of Housing and Environment for the Elderly [in Thai]. Bangkok: Chulalongkorn University, Faculty of Architecture.

Chunharas, S., ed. 2008. *Situation of the Thai Elderly 2007*. Bangkok: Foundation of Thai Gerontology Research and Development Institute (TGRI).

Collin, C., D. T. Wade, S. Davies, and V. Horne. 1998. The Barthel ADL Index: A reliability study. *International Disability Studies*. 10 (2). pp. 61-63.

Donabedian, A. 1985. Twenty Years of Research on the Quality of Medical Care: 1964–1984. *Evaluation & the Health Professions*. 8 (3). pp. 243–65.

Foundation of Thai Gerontology Research and Development Institute (TGRI). 2009. Situation of the Thai Elderly 2008. Bangkok.

———. 2017. Situation of the Thai Elderly 2016. Bangkok.

———. 2019. Situation of the Thai Elderly 2018. Bangkok.

Fries, J.F. 2003. Measuring and Monitoring Success in Compressing Morbidity. *Annals of Internal Medicine.* 139 (5, Part 2). pp. 455–459.

Harman, G. 1996. *Quality Assurance for Higher Education: Developing and Managing Quality Assurance for Higher Education Systems and Institutions in Asia and the Pacific.* Bangkok: United Nations Educational, Scientific and Cultural Organization (UNESCO) Principal Regional Office for Asia and the Pacific.

Harrington, C. 2010. Nursing Home Staffing Standards in State Statutes and Regulations. San Francisco: University of California San Francisco, Department of Social and Behavioral Sciences.

Huguet, J.W., ed. 2014. *Thailand Migrant Report 2014.* Bangkok: United Nations Thematic Working Group on Migration in Thailand.

Japan International Cooperation Agency (JICA). 2018. The Challenge of an Aging Society in Asia: The JICA Approach to Long-term Care; Welfare Services for the Elderly. Tokyo.

Jitapunkul, S., N. Chayovan, and J. Kespichayawattana. 2002. National Policies on Ageing and Long-Term Care Provision for Older Persons in Thailand. In D.R. Phillips and A.C.M. Chan, eds. *Ageing and Long-Term Care: National Policies in the Asia-Pacific.* Singapore: Institute of Southeast Asian Studies; Ottawa: International Development Research Centre. pp. 181–213.

Jitapunkul, S., and S. Wivatvanit. 2009. National Policies and Programs for the Aging Population in Thailand. *Ageing International.* 33. pp. 62–74.

Jitsuchon, S. 2012. Thailand in a Middle-Income Trap. *TDRI Quarterly Review.* 27 (2). pp. 13–20.

———. 2014. *Stability Growth: Fiscal Rules and Good Governance.* Paper presented at the Thailand Development Research Institute (TDRI) Annual Conference 2014: Positioning Thailand in the Next Three Decades; Four Challenges to Quality Growth. Bangkok. 22 November.

Kasemsup, V., T. Sakunphanit, K. Bundhamcharoen, S. Nipaporn, and R. Tansirisithikul. 2016. Thai Country Case Study. In V. Yiengprugsawan, J. Healy, and H. Kendig,eds. *Health System Responses to Population Ageing and Noncommunicable Diseases in Asia. Comparative Country Studies.* 2 (2). pp. 76–110. New Delhi: WHO, Regional Office for South-East Asia (on behalf of the Asia Pacific Observatory on Health Systems and Policies).

Knodel, J., V. Prachuabmoh, and N. Chayovan. 2013. *The Changing Well-Being of Thai Elderly: An Update from the 2011 Survey of Older Persons in Thailand.* Chiang Mai: HelpAge International.

Knodel, J., B. Teerawichitchainan, V. Prachuabmoh, and W. Pothisiri. 2015. The Situation of Thailand's Older Population: An Update Based on the 2014 Survey of Older Persons in Thailand. *Research Collection School of Social Sciences.* Paper 1948. Singapore: Singapore Management University.

Lloyd-Sherlock, P., A.M. Pot, S. Sasat, and F. Morales-Martinez. 2017. Volunteer Provision of Long-Term Care for Older People in Thailand and Costa Rica. *Bulletin of the World Health Organization.* 95 (11). pp. 774–78.

Lloyd-Sherlock, P., S. Sasat, A. Sanee, Y. Miyoshi, and S.H. Lee. 2020. The Rapid Expansion of Residential Long-Term Care Services in Bangkok: A Challenge for Regulation. *University of East Anglia Working Paper Series.* 55. January. Norwich, United Kingdom: University of East Anglia, School of International Development.

Ministry of Commerce, Department of Business Development. 2017. *Number of Establishments for Elderly Care.* Bangkok.

Ministry of Public Health (MOPH). 2018. Report on Public Health Resources 2018 [in Thai]. Nonthaburi, Thailand.

MOPH, Subcommittee on the Deployment and Reform of the Health System for Health Financing and Social Health Protection. 2016. Report on the Deployment and Reform of the Health System for Health Financing and Social Health Protection: Phase 2. Nonthaburi, Thailand: MOPH.

National Committee on Welfare Extension. 2009. Regulations of the National Committee on Welfare Extension on the Standard of Social Welfare. Bangkok.

National Health Commission Office (NHCO): Thailand, Second National Health Assembly. 2009. *Development of Long-term Care for Dependent Elderly People.* Nonthaburi, Thailand.

National Health Security Office (NHSO). 2007. Fund Management Manual of National Health Security. Nonthaburi, Thailand.

————. 2016a. *Manual for the Administration of Health Care in Long-Term Care Services for Older People Living with Dependency under the Universal Health Coverage Scheme* [in Thai]. Bangkok.

————. 2016b. Proclamation of the National Health Security Office on Criteria for Supporting the Administration of a Local Authority on the Local Health Security Fund (Revision 2). Bangkok.

National Reform Council of Thailand. 2015. Reform Agenda No. 30: Reform System for Mitigation of Aging Society [in Thai]. Bangkok.

National Statistical Office (NSO). 2018. *Report on the 2017 Survey of the Older Persons in Thailand* [in Thai]. Bangkok.

————. "Population and Housing Census 1990, 2000, and 2010." http://web.nso.go.th/en/census/poph/cen_poph.htm (accessed 5 April 2020).

Office of the National Economic and Social Development Board (NESDB). 2011. Population Census 2010 and Population Projection. Bangkok.

————. 2013. Population Projections for Thailand 2010–2040. Bangkok.

————. 2017. National Economic and Social Development Plan 12 (2017–2021). Bangkok.

Office of the Prime Minister, Office of the National Economic and Social Development. 2017. Twelfth National Economic and Social Development Plan (2017–2021). Bangkok. https://www.greengrowthknowledge.org/sites/default/files/downloads/policy-database/THAILAND%29%20The%20Twelfth%20National%20Economic%20and%20Social%20Development%20Plan%20%282017-2021%29.pdf.

Okumoto, Y. 2015. *Responding to Ageing Society in Asia: JICA's Work and Experience*. Tokyo: JICA, Office for Gender Equality and Poverty Reduction. https://jaww.info/okumotoRespondingtoageingsocietyinAsia150310new.pdf.

Peek, C., W. Im-em, and R. Tangthanaseth. 2016. *The State of Thailand's Population 2015: Features of Thai Families in the Era of Low Fertility and Longevity*. Bangkok: United Nations Population Fund (UNFPA), Thailand Country Office, and the NESDB.

Prachuabmoh, V. 2008. Design Monitor and Evaluation of the Second National Plan for Older Persons 2001–2021 [in Thai]. Bangkok.

———. 2015. A Lesson Learned from Community-Based Integrated Long-Term Care in Thailand. *Asia Pacific Journal of Social Work and Development*. 25 (4). pp. 213–24.

Prasitsiriphon, O., F. Jeger, A. Tharachompoo, and T. Sakunphanit. 2013. *Costing Model for Long-Term Care System in Thailand*. Bangkok: Health System Research Office.

Pratruangkrai, P. 2016. "Thailand Can Be Centre for Elderly Care." *The Nation Thailand*, 18 July. https://www.nationthailand.com/business/30290874.

Sasat, S. 2012. *Quality of Care Development for Dependent Older Persons in Long-Term Care Institution: Knowledge, Attitude and Practice of Nursing Staff*. Bangkok.

Sasat, S., T. Choowattanapakorn, and P. Lertrat. 2009. *A Model of Institutional Long-Term Care for Older Persons in Thailand*. Nonthaburi, Thailand: Health Systems Research Institute of Thailand.

Sasat, S., T. Choowattanapakorn, T. Pukdeeprom, P. Lertrat, and P. Arunsang. 2009. *Research Report on Long-Term Care Institutions in Thailand*. Nonthaburi, Thailand: Health Systems Research Institute of Thailand.

———. 2013. Long-Term Care Institutions in Thailand. *Journal of Health Research*. 27 (6). pp. 413–18.

Sasat, S., and V. Chuangwiwat. 2013. *Approaches to Home and Community Care Programme for Older People: Thailand Experience*. Paper prepared for the Asia-Pacific Expert Meeting on Long-term Care and China/ESCAP "Strengthening National Capacity for Promoting and Protecting the Rights of Older Persons" Project Launching Meeting. Shanghai. 18–19 December.

Sasat, S., N. Pagaiya, and W. Wisesrith. 2015. *Estimates, Expectations, and Trends in Health Workforce to Support the Aging Society in Thailand*. Nonthaburi, Thailand.

Sasat, S., and T. Pukdeeprom. 2009. Nursing Home. *Journal of Population Studies*. 25 (1). pp. 45–62.

Sasat, S., and W. Wisesrith. 2013. *Estimated Time Spent Caring for Dependent Older Persons*. Bangkok.

Sasat, S., W. Wisesrith, T. Sakunphanit, and R. Soonthornchaiya. 2015. The Development of Care Standard and Service Guideline for Dependent Older Persons in Long-Term Care Institutions in Thailand [in Thai]. Bangkok.

Schmitt, V., T. Sakunphanit, and O. Prasitsiriphol. 2013. *Social Protection Assessment Based National Dialogue: Towards a Nationally Defined Social Protection Floor in Thailand*. Bangkok: International Labour Organization (ILO) and the United Nations Country Team in Thailand.

Singh, D.A. 2016. *Effective Management of Long-Term Care Facilities*. Third edition. Burlington, MA: Jones & Bartlett Learning.

Srithamrongsawat, S. 2017. National Consultation on the Country Diagnostic Study Draft for Thailand. Presentation of an evaluation of community-based long-term care implementation in Thailand. 15 September.

———. 2018. *Experience of Thailand LTC System Development*. Paper presented at the Indonesia National Workshop on LTC Strategy, organized by the Ministry of Planning and ADB. Jakarta. 25–27 April.

Srithamrongsawat, S., and K. Bundhamcharoen. 2010. *Synthesis of Long-Term Care System for the Elderly in Thailand*. Bangkok: TGRI.

Srithamrongsawat, S., K. Bundhamcharoen, S. Sasat, P. Odton, and S. Ratkjaroenkhajorn. 2009. *Projection of Demand and Expenditure for Institutional Long Term Care in Thailand*. Bangkok: Health Insurance System Research Office.

State of California, Department of Health Care Services. *A Report to the California Legislature on Nursing Staff Requirements and the Quality of Nursing Home Care*. Sacramento: Department of Health Care Services.

Suwanrada, W., D. Chalermwong, W. Damjuti, S. Kamruangrit, J. Boonma, and J. Bousquet. 2010. Long-Term Care System for Old-Age Security Promotion [in Thai]. Bangkok: Ministry of Social Development and Human Security, Office of the Welfare Promotion Protection and Empowerment of Vulnerable Groups.

Suwanrada, W., W. Pothisiri, S. Siriboon, B. Bangkaew, and C. Milintangul. 2016. Evaluation of the Replication Project of the Elderly Home Care Volunteers [in Thai]. Bangkok: College of Population Studies, Chulalongkorn University.

Suwanrada, W., S. Sasat, and S. Kamruangrit. 2009. "Financing Long Term Care Services for the Elderly in the Bangkok Metropolitan Administration." Research report submitted to the TGRI and to the Thai Health Promotion Foundation, Bangkok.

Suwanrada, W., S. Sasat, and S. Kumruangrit. 2010. Demand for Long-Term Care Service for Older Persons in Bangkok. *Journal of Economic and Public Policy*. 1 (1). pp. 20–41.

Thai National Working Group. 2019. Thai National Health Accounts 2016. Nonthaburi, Thailand: International Health Policy Foundation (IHPF) and the NHSO. http://www.ihppthaigov.net/wp-content/uploads/2019/09/NHA-report-2016.pdf.

Thailand Development Research Center. 2015. Revenue Sources for Thai Health Care System: Macroeconomic Perspective; Analysis and Synthesis of Academic Work for Sustainable Financing Health System in Thailand [in Thai]. Bangkok.

Thammatacharee, N., K. Tisayaticom, R. Suphanchaimat, S. Limwattananon, W. Putthasri, R. Netsaengtip, and V. Tangcharoensathien. 2012. Prevalence and Profiles of Unmet Healthcare Need in Thailand. Bangkok. *BMC Public Health*. 12. 923.

United Nations Economic and Social Commission for Asia and the Pacific (ESCAP). 2016. *Disability at a Glance 2015: Strengthening Employment Prospects for Persons with Disabilities in Asia and the Pacific*. Bangkok.

United Nations, Population Division. 2019 Revision of World Population Prospects. https://population .un.org/wpp/ (accessed 5 April 2020).

World Bank. Population Density (People per Sq. Km of Land Area). https://data. worldbank.org/indicator/ EN.POP.DNST (accessed 20 March 2017).

———. DataBank: World Development Indicators. https://databank.worldbank.org/source/world-development- indicators (accessed 9 April 2020).

World Bank Group. 2020. *Thailand Economic Monitor, January 2020: Productivity for Prosperity*. Bangkok.

World Health Organization (WHO). 2006. *World Health Report–Working Together for Health*. Geneva.

———. 2007. *Global Age-Friendly Cities: A Guide*. Geneva.

———. 2015. *World Report on Ageing and Health*. Geneva.

———. 2019. *World Health Statistics 2019: Monitoring Health for the SDGs, Sustainable Development Goals*. Geneva.

Yang, J., S. Wang, B. Hansl, S. Zaidi, and P.K. Milne. 2020. Taking the Pulse of Poverty and Inequality in Thailand [in English]. Washington, DC: World Bank Group.

Yodpet, S., L. Sombat, N. Salabol, and T. Sakdaporn. 2012. Operation and Activities of Elderly Clubs [in Thai]. Bangkok: TGRI and the Thai Health Foundation.

Yotphet, S., L. Sombat, P. Chockthanawanit, and T. Sakdaporn. 2009. Model of Good Practice in Caring for Older Persons by Family and Rural Community in Thailand. Bangkok: TGRI and the Health Systems Research Institute of Thailand.

www.ingramcontent.com/pod-product-compliance
Lightning Source LLC
Chambersburg PA
CBHW051657210326
41518CB00026B/2610